Power and Corporate Responsibility

T0271159

Power and Corporate Responsibility explores the concept of corporate responsibility and offers a systematic discussion by referring to the following dimensions: understanding responsibility, taking responsibility, governing responsibility, managing responsibility, investing in responsibility, reporting on responsibility and regulating responsibility.

The aim of the book is to provide a user-friendly but theoretically grounded overview of the core dimensions of CR. The seven dimensions of CR are not offered as a definitive framework, but rather a flexible conceptual framework that is compatible with acknowledged thought leadership in the field. The author uses his diverse academic background, as well as his practitioner background, to debunk some of the myths associated with CSR using mini case studies, but also to illustrate the strategic importance of the concept of CR.

This accessible book will be a valuable resource for business management scholars, instructors and upper-level students, and those with a particular interest in business ethics, CSR and corporate governance. It will also serve as a guide for participants in executive education courses.

Daniel Malan is the director of the Trinity Corporate Governance Lab at Trinity College Dublin, Ireland. He was a co-chair of the Business 20 (B20) Task Force on Integrity and Compliance (2022 and 2020) and is a former member of the Global Future Council on Transparency and Anti-Corruption of the World Economic Forum (2019–2022). He holds a PhD in business administration, a master's degree in philosophy as well as a master's degree in business administration (MBA) from Stellenbosch University, South Africa.

Routledge CoBS Focus on Responsible Business
Series Editors
Tom Gamble and Adrian Zicari
The Council on Business and Society (CoBS)

This series is published in collaboration with the Council on Business & Society (COBS).

Routledge COBS Focus on Responsible Business provides international and multicultural perspectives on responsible leadership and business practices in line with the UN SDGs. Contributors from leading business schools on 4 continents offer local, cultural and global perspectives on the issues covered, drawing on high level research and transformed into engaging, and digestible content for students, academics and practitioners.

Topics include but are not limited to; responsible finance and accounting, CSR and governance, supply chain management, leadership, diversity and inclusion, performance and innovation, responsible management, and wellbeing at work.

Responsible Finance and Accounting
Performance and Profit for Better Business, Society and Planet
Edited by Adrián Zicari and Tom Gamble

Power and Corporate Responsibility

Dimensions, Purpose and Value

Daniel Malan

Routledge
Taylor & Francis Group

LONDON AND NEW YORK

First published 2024
by Routledge
4 Park Square, Milton Park, Abingdon, Oxon OX14 4RN

and by Routledge
605 Third Avenue, New York, NY 10158

Routledge is an imprint of the Taylor & Francis Group, an informa business

© 2024 Daniel Malan

British Library Cataloguing-in-Publication Data
A catalogue record for this book is available from the British Library

ISBN: 978-1-032-41239-9 (hbk)
ISBN: 978-1-032-41240-5 (pbk)
ISBN: 978-1-003-35698-1 (ebk)

DOI: 10.4324/9781003356981

Typeset in Times New Roman
by Apex CoVantage, LLC

Dedicated to my parents.

Contents

Tables

Figures

Acknowledgements

There have been many people who have played different roles in shaping my somewhat eclectic career. It is always risky to name individuals, but the most important ones include:

- From my student days and early career: Johan Degenaar, Willie Esterhuyse, Willie van der Merwe, Wolfgang Thomas, Petrus Marais and Eon Smit
- From my academic career: Tom Donaldson, Bob Garratt, Martin Hilb and Oliver Williams

Tom Donaldson has been the most influential in the development of my own thoughts, and much of the content of this book relies on his pioneering work in the field of business ethics. He is a giant in academia but has not received enough recognition from the world of practitioners in terms of the potential impact of his work. While I cannot do justice to the intellectual scope and sophistication of his contribution, if this book can help in some small way to increase the impact of his work I will be satisfied.

I acknowledge the support of Stellenbosch Business School in South Africa and Trinity Business School in Ireland. The book is based on my PhD dissertation that was submitted to Stellenbosch University. My involvement with the World Economic Forum and the Business 20 (B20) has given me valuable insights into the priorities and thought processes of the international business community.

I would like to thank the Council on Business & Society for their support, as well as the Rijksmuseum in Amsterdam for their permission to use two images from their collection.

And finally, to my wife, Lize, and my daughters, Tessa and Greta: I cannot describe how much you mean to me, so I will not even try.

1 Introduction

More than 350 years ago the Dutch painter Jan Asselijn produced one of his most famous paintings, *The Threatened Swan*. In this painting a hissing swan defends the eggs in her nest against an approaching and seemingly aggressive dog.

Later owners of the painting added inscriptions by painting labels (in Dutch) directly onto the canvas: the dog was referred to as the "enemy of the state", the swan was labelled the "pensionary", a reference to the position of principal public servant in the Dutch provinces, and the eggs under threat were labelled "Holland". These rather crude additions to the painting – akin to graffiti – give a specific interpretation to the more generic "good versus evil" symbolism that was probably the original intention of the painter. Involuntarily, we feel tempted to substitute our own inscriptions: who in our contemporary society would represent the dog, the swan and the eggs?

The inscriptions are barely visible on the reproduced image. They were added within a particular context and referred to a specific individual, Johan de Witt, whose family emblem was a swan. De Witt was the pensionary at the time and instrumental in defending the interests of Holland against England.

Anybody who visits Amsterdam should plan to visit the Rijksmuseum and to have a look at the original painting. It is mesmerizing. When I saw it for the first time I was preoccupied with thoughts about ethics and responsibility, and for me the painting has become an allegory for corporate responsibility.

The eggs become much more than Holland – they represent our fragile society which comprises a vast, globalised network of corporations, governments and civil society. At the moment, there are regions in the world, including Ukraine, where conflict is rampant and human suffering and economic decline are visible to all. But if nurtured properly, the eggs have the potential to hatch and grow. The swan has a dual responsibility – to protect the eggs from outside threats, and to guide the young, once hatched, to fulfil their true potential. Within a global environment, the closest equivalent to a principal public servant is the United Nations (UN) – a body comprising representatives

DOI: 10.4324/9781003356981-1

Figure 1.1 The Threatened Swan by Jan Asselijn, circa 1650
Source: Courtesy of Rijksmuseum Amsterdam

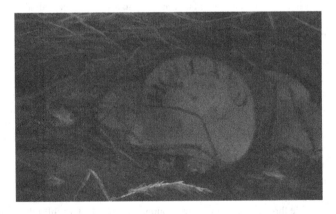

Figure 1.2 Detail from *The Threatened Swan* by Jan Asselijn, circa 1650
Source: Courtesy of Rijksmuseum Amsterdam

from 193 nations of the world, with the ability to protect sovereignty (e.g. through peacekeeping forces), and to guide action (e.g. through conventions, treaties and also through its own corporate responsibility initiative, the UN Global Compact). And the dog? The dog remains the enemy of states, societies and organisations – it represents a multiplicity of aggressive and negative forces, ranging from excessive greed and corruption to disrespect for and abuse of basic human rights and the natural environment. In the words of former UN Secretary-General Kofi Annan when he announced the formation of the Global Compact in 1999 (United Nations, 1999), "the global economy [is] vulnerable to backlash from all the 'isms' of our post-cold-war world: protectionism; populism; nationalism; ethnic chauvinism; fanaticism; and terrorism".

A closer look at *The Threatened Swan* reveals a few more interesting aspects that are relevant here. Firstly, the date of the painting is unknown, but it was painted at the time when early multinationals such as the Dutch East India Company and the British charter companies were expanding their operations globally.

Secondly, the painting highlights how economic considerations often influence our actions and how this can have an impact over the long term. In its commentary on the painting, the Rijksmuseum in Amsterdam explains that painters sometimes used a combination of cheap and expensive paints in order to save money. This is also the case with *The Threatened Swan*. The sky behind the swan was painted with expensive paint and has remained bright until today, while the rest of the painting has become faded and grey over time as a consequence of the use of a cheaper paint. So, the austerity measures implemented by Asselijn have resulted in a somewhat faded painting, but without those measures the painting might never have been produced at all. To restore the painting to its former glory, we therefore require a pigment of the imagination!

Thirdly, the overlay of words and images produced by different people does not only invite different interpretations but illustrates the attempts by the written word to capture and represent reality. This is particularly relevant for discussions about corporate reporting. In Umberto Eco's discussion of the limitations of interpretation (Eco, 1990: 1), he quotes from *The Secret and Swift Messenger* by John Wilkins, who in 1641 – about the same time that the inscriptions were added to *The Threatened Swan* – wrote about a slave who was accused of stealing because of information contained in a letter. This was written almost 400 years ago and therefore should be interpreted within a context where slavery was acceptable. The language itself reflects the different context and is worth quoting at length:

How strange a thing this Art of Writing did seem at its first Invention, we may guess by the late discovered Americans, who were amazed to see Men converse with Books, and could scarce make themselves to believe that a Paper could speak. . . . There is a pretty Relation to this Purpose, concerning an Indian Slave; who being sent by his Master with a Basket of Figs and a Letter, did by the Way eat up a great Part of his Carriage, conveying the Remainder unto the Person to whom he was directed; who when he read the Letter, and not finding the Quantity of Figs answerable to what was spoken of, he accuses the Slave of eating them, telling him what the Letter said against him. But the Indian (notwithstanding this Proof) did confidently abjure the Fact, cursing the Paper, as being a false and lying Witness. After this, being sent again with the like carriage, and a Letter expressing the just Number of Figs, that were to be delivered, he did again, according to his former Practice, devour a great Part of them by the Way; but before meddled with any, (to prevent all following Accusations) he first took the Letter, and hid that under a great Stone, assuring himself, that if it did not see him eating the Figs, it could never tell of him; but being now more strongly accused than before, he confesses the Fault, admiring the Divinity of the Paper, and for the future does promise his best Fidelity in every employment.

We should therefore be mindful that documents – whether they are ancient philosophical treatises or glossy corporate publications – are interpretations and are at least one step removed from actions that could change the world for better or for worse. Of course, that is also true of this book.

Finally, the image of the swan in business writing is more often associated with the phenomenon of the black swan, a metaphor for an unexpected and high-impact event, usually with negative consequences. The most relevant contemporary commentary on this topic is the work of Nassim Taleb, with reference to his work from 2007, *The Black Swan: The Impact of the Highly Improbable*. To illustrate the phenomenon, he quotes the words of a famous ship's captain:

> But in all my experience, I have never been in any accident . . . of any sort worth speaking about. I have seen but one vessel in distress in all my years at sea. I never saw a wreck and never have been wrecked nor was I ever in any predicament that threatened to end in disaster of any sort.

These words were allegedly spoken in 1907 by E.J. Smith, captain of the ill-fated RMS *Titanic*, approximately five years before the ship sank.[1]

---

1 www.goodreads.com/work/quotes/2157806-the-black-swan-the-impact-of-the-highly-improbable, accessed 26 November 2014.

A final reflection on Asselijn's painting leads to a number of questions that will be addressed in this book:

- Who does the dog represent, and who the swan? For the Dutch it might have been quite obvious in the seventeenth century that the English were the "enemy of the state", but the English probably held exactly the same view about the Dutch. When we talk about morality and values, is it possible – with such opposing perspectives in mind – to develop consensus on what is right and what is wrong, and how organisations should behave?
- How can the swan know the best way to protect her eggs? Should she spend more time defending against the dog, or should she spend more time helping the chicks to grow strong and protect themselves? Regulators around the world and in different disciplines are faced with this decision every day: to what extent can organisations be trusted (or incentivized) to do the right thing, and to what extent does one need to force them to do what is required?
- On what information does the swan base her actions? The dog has been labelled an enemy of the state and is possibly acting aggressively, but what would have happened if the dog had a friendlier countenance and approached in a less threatening manner? We receive our information from reports, media releases, video clips, social media, etc. All of these have been prepared consciously and with the explicit aim to bring across a particular message. Even a factual report that has been verified by an accounting firm conveys one intended message rather than another. And of course, in the age of artificial intelligence, we often simply don't even know whether there was human involvement in the production of a report.
- How does the swan balance her various responsibilities? Keeping an eye on the dog, protecting the eggs from other possible dangers, finding food for herself and resting. These can be understood as governance issues and require careful thinking and a full understanding of the possible implications of various courses of action.

This book will explore power and corporate responsibility by looking specifically at two concepts: purpose and value. This will be done by suggesting six separate but related dimensions of responsibility. It is argued that organisations that embrace the proposed framework will become more responsible and more successful in a rapidly changing global environment.

Ts and Cs apply

We are often warned by the words "terms and conditions apply" that things are not as straightforward as they might seem. This is also the case here. Theories and concepts should be applied. Before we can look at the proposed framework for responsibility, it is necessary to contextualise the topic and the views that will be presented. It is also necessary for the reader to take a step back and reconsider – critically – whether their previous or current views remain valid.

At the most basic level, the way in which we view the world (and the role of business in the world) is framed by a theoretical approach (how do we understand it?) and a practitioner's approach (how do we change it?), as depicted in Figure 1.3. Although related, this distinction is not the same as the philosophical distinction between ontology (what exists?) and epistemology (what can we know about things that exist?).

The theoretical approach may be either normative, prescribing what ought to be done, or it may be empirical, describing the way things are. Each of these views of the theoretical approach presents significant challenges and complexities. In brief, the normative view is often accused of being idealistic and not in touch with the business environment. The empirical approach is sometimes challenged because it does not grapple with the difficult ethical issues implicit in a business environment, and also because the large amounts of quantitative data associated with empirical investigation and the positive correlations between the data do not necessarily prove causation. From a business practitioner's perspective there are many interventions and initiatives that can assist companies to make an impact, for example voluntary initiatives such as the UN Global Compact or other industry agreements. These initiatives are often accused of using theoretical sleight of hand to sidestep the choice between the business case (we do things, including acting with integrity, because we will make more money) and the moral case (we do things because they are the right things to do, whether we will make more money or not). This sleight

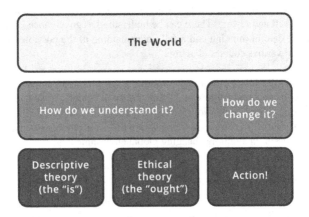

Figure 1.3 Understanding and changing the world

of hand is represented by the enlightened self-interest approach (we do things because they are the right things to do, and, fortunately for us, they are also good for business). As will be illustrated later, this approach has theoretical limitations and is unfortunately also often associated with lip service.

These are the Ts and Cs that apply for a reading of this book:

- Both human beings and organisations form part of broader society, both are shaped by society and have an impact on society through their actions. Therefore, both have responsibilities to align their actions with universal ethical principles (this is a normative assumption and will be discussed in detail with regard to the moral purpose of business).
- As human beings – whether we represent the interests of other people or organisations or simply look out for ourselves – we have a wide variety of views on just about everything, and consensus on almost all of these is both impossible and unnecessary; sufficient consensus is the minimum requirement for cooperation among different stakeholder groups, and that *is* achievable.
- This diversity of opinion also applies to our sense of what is right and wrong. As humans, we all have that sense, and although there is remarkable similarity about the big-ticket items, there is sufficient disagreement to keep a conversation going that is already a few thousand years old.
- When human beings make judgements on moral issues, they assess not only the activities of individuals but also ask whether corporations or states can act in an ethical manner, and they often question the acceptability of the system within which they operate. Views on ethical behaviour and ethical responsibilities will therefore focus on individuals (e.g. Bernie Madoff, Ken Lay or Elon Musk), on corporations (e.g. Enron, Volkswagen or Meta), and on systems (e.g. capitalism, socialism or hybrid versions of the two).
- The term "corporate responsibility" (CR), rather than "corporate social responsibility" (CSR), is preferred in this book. This is in line with an international trend, which is based loosely on the realisation that there is a need for a more comprehensive description of corporate responsibility rather than merely a reference to the societal aspects. Furthermore, the use of the term "corporate social responsibility" can have the unintentional effect of positioning the corporation as something separate from broader society. And finally, given the history of CSR, many commentators still associate the term CSR with peripheral, philanthropic activities, rather than something that is integrated into the core strategy of the corporation. To a limited extent, the terms "CR", "CSR" and "corporate citizenship" can be used interchangeably, and, when they appear in certain literature, can also be interpreted as such, unless there is a specific comment to the contrary.

Sustainability

Although this book does not focus extensively on the concept of sustainability, it forms an integral part of discussions about corporate responsibility. In 1987 the UN's Brundtland Report defined sustainable development as "development which meets the need of the present without compromising the ability of future generations to meet their own needs". This definition has become so ubiquitous that people often use the phrase glibly without understanding the underlying motivations and implications. A closer look at the original paragraph is therefore useful (United Nations, 1987: 16):

> Humanity has the ability to make development sustainable to ensure that it meets the needs of the present without compromising the ability of future generations to meet their own needs. The concept of sustainable development does imply limits – not absolute limits but limitations imposed by the present state of technology and social organization on environmental resources and by the ability of the biosphere to absorb the effects of human activities. But technology and social organization can be both managed and improved to make way for a new era of economic growth. The Commission believes that widespread poverty is no longer inevitable. Poverty is not only an evil in itself, but sustainable development requires meeting the basic needs of all and extending to all the opportunity to fulfil their aspirations for a better life. A world in which poverty is endemic will always be prone to ecological and other catastrophes.

The following paragraph (my emphasis added) is of particular importance (United Nations, 1987: 17):

> [S]ustainable development is not a fixed state of harmony, but rather *a process of change* in which the exploitation of resources, the direction of investments, the orientation of technological development, and institutional change are made consistent with future as well as present needs. We do not pretend that the process is easy or straightforward. *Painful choices* have to be made. Thus, in the final analysis, sustainable development must rest on *political will*.

The Brundtland Report is particularly clear about the fact that sustainable development does not refer to environmental issues in isolation – this is a mistake that is often made (United Nations, 1987: 7):

> The environment does not exist as a sphere separate from human actions, ambitions, and needs, and attempts to defend it in isolation from human concerns have given the very word "environment" a connotation of naivety in some political circles.

A limitation of this book is that it has been written from a Western philosophical perspective. Claims about universal values and the construction of a social contract are part of this tradition and form part of the intellectual lens that has shaped this work. Of course, the pluralistic nature of this tradition opens the door for external challenges and critical debates about the fundamental framework, but that in itself is part of the perspective and could potentially also be challenged by other philosophical paradigms. This limitation is acknowledged but will not be explored further in this book.

The book is structured as follows:

- Chapter 2 describes the overall conceptual framework for corporate responsibility.
- Chapter 3 focuses on understanding responsibility, with specific reference to the related concepts of power, purpose and value.
- Chapter 4 focuses on taking responsibility with specific reference to ethical leadership.
- Chapter 5 focuses on the related but different activities of governance and management.
- Chapter 6 focuses on the rapidly developing field of corporate reporting, with specific reference to sustainability reporting and integrated reporting.
- Chapter 7 focuses on the regulation of responsibility, with specific reference to the distinction between voluntary and mandatory standards.

References

Eco, U. 1990. *The limits of interpretation.* Bloomington: Indiana University Press.

Taleb, N. 2007. *The Black Swan: The impact of the highly improbable.* London: Penguin Books.

United Nations. 1987. *Our common future.* [Online] Available: www.un-documents. net/our-common-future.pdf Accessed: 7 December 2014.

United Nations. 1999. *Secretary-general proposes global compact on human rights, labour, environment, in address to world economic forum in Davos.* [Online] Available: www.un.org/press/en/1999/19990201.sgsm6881.html Accessed: 14 June 2015.

2 A conceptual framework for corporate responsibility

The main purpose of this book is to present a conceptual framework that could be applied to improve the effectiveness of corporate responsibility initiatives. In a multidisciplinary environment where context is critical, this is no easy task. The intention is to guide thinking and actions, not to provide solutions. The framework is conceptual and based on theory that will be introduced in the next chapter.

The framework is not offered as a complete solution – that would contradict the context-based approach that is followed. The framework provides practical, yet theoretically grounded, guidelines to any organisation, regardless of its size, location or industry.

The framework is both modest and ambitious: modest, because it is based on existing theory with only slight adaptations suggested within a corporate responsibility context; ambitious, because it attempts to cover the elusive divide between academic theory and the world of practitioners. As will be seen, much of the content has been inspired by the work of Tom Donaldson from the Wharton School at the University of Pennsylvania. Donaldson is one of the giants of the business ethics field, and his influence has been substantial. I was introduced to his work while I was working as an ethics consultant at KPMG, and the theoretical framework of Integrative Social Contracts Theory (Donaldson & Dunfee, 1999) which was already anticipated in earlier contributions (Donaldson & Dunfee, 1994) had a major impact on some of the work I have performed with clients. His later work, first in cooperation with Jim Walsh (Donaldson & Walsh, 2015) and more recently on practical inference (Donaldson, 2021), makes further important contributions.

The book aims to assist corporations to conceptualise, develop and implement effective corporate responsibility programmes. It is underpinned by the need to have a thorough understanding of responsibility, with specific reference to the distinction between the moral and business case for corporate responsibility. Such an understanding then enables the corporation to take responsibility and informs a sequential series of activities that relate to both internal processes (governing responsibility, managing responsibility and

DOI: 10.4324/9781003356981-2

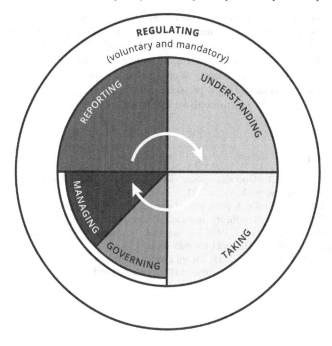

Figure 2.1 A conceptual framework for corporate responsibility

reporting on responsibility), as well as responding to the external activity of
regulating responsibility.

The framework can be summarised as follows. Corporate responsibility
has different dimensions: there is a conceptual side, which involves understanding and taking responsibility, and an operational side, which involves
governing, managing and reporting on responsibility. Taking responsibility
provides the transition from the conceptual side to the operational side. All of
these dimensions are situated within a regulatory framework, which comprises
a combination of mandatory and voluntary requirements. Although there is
a somewhat logical sequence involved (understanding responsibility has to
precede taking responsibility, and performance has to precede reporting), in
practice these dimensions will be addressed concurrently within a business
environment. The regulatory framework is ever-present, and therefore the
mandatory and voluntary standards will also appear on each of the segmented
graphs that will be used in the sections that follow. Some might question the
absence of assurance from the framework. The reason for the omission is
twofold. Firstly, assurance and certification are implicit in some components

of reporting and compliance and, to a more limited extent, in some voluntary standards (e.g. SA 8000 and the ISO 14000 series). Secondly, with regard to corporate responsibility, it is my opinion that the writer's opinion that assurance plays a limited role. This is aligned with the view that stakeholders are the ultimate compliance officers of companies, because they will scrutinise corporate behaviour and apply pressure where required.

In the remainder of this book the different dimensions will be discussed in detail.

References

Donaldson, T. 2021. How values ground value creation: The practical inference framework. *Organization Theory*, 2, 1–27.

Donaldson, T. & Dunfee, T. 1994. Toward a unified conception of business ethics: Integrative social contracts theory. *Academy of Management Review*, 19(2), 252–284.

Donaldson, T. & Dunfee, T. 1999. *Ties that bind: A social contracts approach to business ethics.* Boston: Harvard University Press.

Donaldson, T. & Walsh, J. 2015. Toward a theory of business. *Research in Organizational Behavior*, 35(181–207). doi:10.1016/j.riob.2015.10.002.

3 Understanding responsibility

Society . . . is typically marked by a conflict as well as by an identity of interest. There is an identity of interest since social cooperation makes possible a better life for all than any would have if each were to live solely by [their] own efforts. There is a conflict of interests since persons are not indifferent as to how the greater benefits produced by their collaboration are distributed, for in order to pursue their ends they each prefer a larger to a lesser share.

John Rawls[1]

In a globalised world the corporation is an important and powerful player. Multinational companies often wield more power than the governments of countries where they have operations. Most people are familiar with the comparisons between corporations and companies. According to the UK's Global Justice Now, 157 out of the top 200 economic entities in the world are corporations.[2]

The top 30 "economies" appear in Table 3.1.

The power of corporations can be understood at various levels. Carroll and Buchholtz (2006: 17–18) discuss Epstein's view that there are four main levels, which are closely aligned with discussions about levels of business ethics, as indicated in parentheses: macro (the corporate system), intermediate (industry initiatives), micro (individual firms) and individual (CEOs and other executives). Power is also exerted in various ways, including in the economic, social, cultural, individual, technological, environmental and political spheres (Carroll & Buchholtz, 2006: 18). The way in which this power is exerted introduces the responsibility element: "whenever power and responsibility become substantially out of balance, forces will be generated to bring them in closer balance" (Carroll & Buchholtz, 2006: 19).

---

1 This quote is taken from *A Theory of Justice* (Rawls, 1971: 4)
2 See www.globaljustice.org.uk/news/69-richest-100-entities-planet-are-corporations-not-governments-figures-show/.

DOI: 10.4324/9781003356981-3

Figure 3.1 Understanding responsibility

Table 3.1 Top 30 economies in the world based on 2018 data

Rank	Name	Revenue (USD)	Type
1	United States	3,336,000,000,000	Government
2	China	2,591,000,000,000	Government
3	Japan	1,678,000,000,000	Government
4	Germany	1,598,000,000,000	Government
5	France	1,446,000,000,000	Government
6	United Kingdom	984,400,000,000	Government
7	Italy	884,400,000,000	Government
8	Brazil	819,400,000,000	Government
9	Canada	623,700,000,000	Government
10	**Walmart**	**500,343,000,000**	**Corporation**
11	Spain	492,400,000,000	Government
12	Australia	461,000,000,000	Government
13	**State Grid**	**348,903,000,000**	**Corporation**
14	Netherlands	344,800,000,000	Government
15	**Sinopec Group**	**326,953,000,000**	**Corporation**
16	**China National Petroleum**	**326,008,000,000**	**Corporation**
17	Korea, South	318,000,000,000	Government
18	**Royal Dutch Shell**	**311,870,000,000**	**Corporation**

Rank	Name	Revenue (USD)	Type
19	Mexico	292,800,000,000	Government
20	Sweden	274,800,000,000	Government
21	**Toyota Motor Corporation**	**265,172,000,000**	**Corporation**
22	**Volkswagen**	**260,028,000,000**	**Corporation**
23	Russia	253,900,000,000	Government
24	Belgium	249,700,000,000	Government
25	**BP**	**244,582,000,000**	**Corporation**
26	**Exxon Mobil**	**244,363,000,000**	**Corporation**
27	**Berkshire Hathaway**	**242,137,000,000**	**Corporation**
28	India	229,300,000,000	Government
29	**Apple**	**229,234,000,000**	**Corporation**
30	Switzerland	223,500,000,000	Government

Source: Global Justice Now

Although there is disagreement about whether it was Voltaire or Spiderman who first said "with great power comes great responsibility", many companies use this logic to explain why they feel morally obliged to behave responsibly. But the flip side is also true: with great responsibility comes great power. That is what many companies experience as they rethink their purpose and redefine their corporate responsibility.

The work of Archie Carroll has been instrumental in tracing the history of CSR as well as describing defining moments in its development. Carroll defines CSR as follows (Visser et al., 2007: 122–123):

[It is t]he general belief . . . that modern businesses have responsibilities to society that extend beyond their obligations to the stockholders or investors. . . . [CSR] encompasses the economic, legal, ethical and discretionary/philanthropic expectations that society has of organizations at a given point in time.

Carroll (1999: 270) quotes one of the early definitions of CSR by Bowen, who said in 1953 that CSR refers to "the obligations of businessmen[3] to pursue those policies, to make those decisions, or to follow those lines of action which are desirable in terms of the objectives and the values of our society". Carroll outlined many new concepts that were added over the decades, for example stakeholder theory, business ethics and corporate citizenship. He predicted that increasing attention will be given in the 21st century

---

3 Most earlier contributions in the literature do not use gender-neutral language. Sometimes, in legal language, there is an odd way of addressing this by adding a footnote to the effect that "he" also implies "she", or more recently "they". I will simply call this out once in its historical context as something that could be understood but not condoned.

to measurement initiatives as well as theoretical developments (Carroll, 1999: 292):

> [T]he CSR concept will remain as an essential part of business language and practice, because it is a vital underpinning to many of the other theories and is continually consistent with what the public expects of the business community today.

Looking back at Carroll's predictions, which were made in 1999, it seems that subsequent emphasis was placed more on the development of measurement initiatives than on further theoretical developments. Part of the reason for this development can perhaps be found in the fact that CR has become increasingly mainstream in business *operations* since the turn of the century. Carroll's prediction was published two years before the collapse of Enron and approximately eight years before the onset of the global financial crisis.

In a later contribution, the following definition of corporate responsibility is provided by Carroll et al. (2012: 7): "[T]he idea that the corporation exists in society and has rights and responsibilities as a member (or citizen) of that society." They identify the following recurrent themes in the history of corporate responsibility: the relationship between ethics and corporate responsibility; leadership, organisations and responsibility; stakeholders; sustainability; measurement; power and responsibility; and the concept of a new social contract (Carroll et al., 2012: 17–26).

Williams (2014a: 5–10) traces the history of CSR and discusses the important contributions from many scholars since the 1940s. The definition for CSR proposed by Williams (2014: 5) is "behaviour of business which seeks to solve social problems in the wider society that would not ordinarily be addressed in the pursuit of profits". He discusses the challenge of reconciling and integrating economic and social values, with reference to contributions or suggestions from Mackey ("conscious capitalism"), Gates ("creative capitalism") and Cohen and Greenfield ("caring capitalism") (Williams, 2014: 6). It is interesting to note the use of the words "not ordinarily", because this seems to challenge some of the more strategic approaches to corporate responsibility.

Freeman et al. (2020) mention a few more concepts as part of what they call the new way of thinking about business. For example, they discuss connected capitalism, the rise of the B Corporation and the importance of social entrepreneurship.

Schwab (2008) makes the point that the term CSR is an oversimplification, and then proceeds with a brief conceptual comparison between corporate governance, corporate philanthropy, corporate social responsibility and corporate social entrepreneurship, before introducing the concept of global corporate citizenship. He makes the important point that corporations should not only focus on engagement with their stakeholders, but that they should understand that they themselves *are* stakeholders in a broader process, alongside governments and civil society. He discusses global challenges such as climate change, public health care, energy conservation and water management as particular examples of global priorities that can only be addressed through partnerships between corporations, governments and civil society (Schwab, 2008: 107). As justification for this proposed approach, Schwab (2008: 107) uses the enlightened self-interest argument in way that anticipates the concept of Creating Shared Value:

> Because these global issues increasingly impact business, not to engage with them can hurt the bottom line. Because global citizenship is in a corporation's enlightened self-interest, it is sustainable. Addressing global issues can be good both for the corporation and for society at a time of increasing globalization and diminishing state influence.

With reference to the Ts and Cs discussed earlier, the point is made by Freeman et al. (2010: 235) that most of the discussions about CSR take place from a Western perspective, and they correctly point out that there are also other important examples, for example from countries such as India, China and Japan. They also challenge the notion that the Western form of CSR originated in the 1950s by pointing out that some of the writings of Andrew Carnegie already addressed issues of the relationship between business and society at the beginning of the twentieth century (Freeman et al., 2010: 235). In the view of Freeman et al. (2010: 236), "intentions behind corporate social responsibility are better satisfied if we think about *company stakeholder responsibility*". They object to the use of the word "corporate" because it creates the impression that only large corporations have this responsibility. They also object to the word "social" because it represents an outdated conceptual scheme of separating a corporation's social and business responsibilities (Freeman et al., 2010: 263). The following example illustrates this point eloquently (Freeman et al., 2010: 261–262):

> Assume that the CEO of firm A is asked the following: "Well, I know that your company makes products that consumers like, and that those products make their lives better. And I know that suppliers want to do business with your company because they benefit from the business relationship. I also know that employees really want to work for your company, and are satisfied with their remuneration and professional development. And let's not forget that you're a good citizen in the communities where you are located; among other things, you pay taxes on the profits you make. You compete hard but fairly. You also make an attractive return on capital for shareholders and other financiers. However, are you socially responsible?"

> We confess to having absolutely no idea what "socially responsible" could mean here.

These authors point out, in a discussion on the contribution made by Carroll, that four different categories of social responsibility can be identified which correspond with different expectations from society. These categories were also included in Carroll's definition, discussed earlier. They are (Freeman et al., 2010: 240):

- economic responsibilities: the need to produce goods and services that society wants, and to sell them at a profit;
- legal responsibilities: the need to respect the ground rules under which business is expected to operate;
- ethical responsibilities: additional behaviour that is not a legal requirement but expected by society; and
- discretionary responsibilities: for example, contributions that do not respond to a clearly defined expectation by society.

Enderle (2010) has pointed out that this description does not make provision for environmental issues, and also that it is not very helpful to position ethical responsibilities as something separate from other responsibilities that also have normative components.

Summarising a lively debate that has ensued over many decades is not easy, but the following is an attempt to describe how – in broad terms – different individuals and corporations have viewed CSR over time. There has been a logical development from traditional CSR to strategic CSR/CR. This has coincided with a shift from a focus on how profits are spent to how profits are made. The different approaches can be described as a one-way street (traditional CSR), a two-way street (CSR based on enlightened self-interest) and a virtuous cycle (strategic CSR/CR based on strong moral values). Traditional CSR uses profits to spend on worthy causes, often as a way to offset the way in which the profits were made (the term "guilt money" is sometimes used). This approach is aligned with the discretionary and ethical responsibilities outlined above. Enlightened self-interest is conscious of both risks and opportunities and is therefore strong on stakeholder engagement. However, this approach is mostly opportunistic, and if the business case is not strong enough, corporations might quickly lose interest. Strategic CSR/CR is based on a deep understanding of the purpose of business and the way in which corporations form an integral part of society. Driven by a strong moral commitment and a clear understanding of the nature of the business, contributions are made in such a way that the corporation uses its particular strengths to thrive and contribute to societal needs at the same time. This is not a chequebook approach, but is based on the real capabilities and specific expertise of the corporation. Strategic CSR/CR achieves integration on two fronts. Firstly, so-called CSR

Profit — TRADITIONAL CSR → One-way street: Philanthropic spend

Profit ← ENLIGHTENED SELF-INTEREST → Two-way street: Spend based on stakeholder engagement, informed by risk and opportunity

Profit — STRATEGIC CSR/CR — Virtuous cycle: Spend based on overlap between societal needs, business opportunities and ethical values

Figure 3.2 Different approaches to corporate responsibility

activities are no longer peripheral but are integrated into the core activities of the corporation. Secondly, the business case and moral case are not presented as part of an either/or choice (see Figure 3.2).

Power and purpose

Very few, if any, corporations would today still adhere to the views expressed by Milton Friedman in his famous article that was originally published in the *New York Times Magazine* in 1970 (Friedman, 2002). In this article, Friedman argues that the only social responsibility of business is to increase its profits (Friedman, 2002: 33):

> [B]usinessmen [who] believe that they are defending free enterprise when they declaim that business is not concerned 'merely' with profit but also with promoting desirable 'social' ends; that business has a 'social conscience' and takes seriously its responsibilities for providing employment, eliminating discrimination, avoiding pollution and whatever else may be the catchword of the contemporary crop of reformers . . . are . . . preaching pure and unadulterated socialism.

Friedman's views were echoed by the philosopher John Ladd, quoted by Goodpaster and Matthews (1982: 133):

> We cannot and must not expect formal organizations, or their representatives acting in their official capacities, to be honest, courageous, considerate,

sympathetic, or to have any kind of moral integrity. Such concepts are not in the vocabulary, so to speak, of the organizational language game.

However, implicit in Friedman's argument is the view that corporations *could* engage in some of these activities, as long as they do it because they believe that it will increase their profits and not because of a moral obligation. Consider the following less familiar paragraph from the very same article (Friedman, 2002: 36):

> It may well be in the long run interest of a corporation that is a major employer in a small community to devote resources to providing amenities to that community or to improving its government. That may make it easier to attract desirable employees, it may reduce the wage bill or lessen losses from pilferage and sabotage or have other worthwhile effects.

This type of argument resonates very strongly with the current risk-based approach to corporate responsibility and more specifically with the creating shared value (CSV) concept introduced by Porter and Kramer (2011), discussed below. In terms of a risk-based approach, corporations should take their social responsibilities seriously because it will assist them to manage risks and exploit opportunities and will therefore be in their own interest.

We have seen major shifts in how the traditional business media has dealt with corporate responsibility. Following a fairly scathing review of corporate social responsibility by *The Economist* (The good company: A survey of corporate social responsibility, 2005), a follow-up report was published in 2008 by *The Economist*, where it refers to the fact that the 2005 report "acknowledge[d], with regret, that the CSR movement had won the battle of ideas" (*The Economist*, 2008: 4). Whether this regret had anything to do with Friedman's views of CSR as unadulterated socialism is not clear, but the 2008 report – as indicated by the title of "Just Good Business" – acknowledges, with no regret this time, that "clearly CSR has arrived" (*The Economist*, 2008: 4). It then proceeds to explain how companies should view this development (*The Economist*, 2008: 14):

> One way of looking at CSR is that it is part of what businesses need to do to keep up with (or, if possible, stay slightly ahead of) society's fast-changing expectations. It is an aspect of taking care of a company's reputation, managing its risks and gaining a competitive edge. This is what good managers ought to do anyway.

But there is a twist in the tail. Those who support corporate responsibility from a moral point of view increasingly support the "just good business" approach from an *operational* point of view. In other words, by integrating corporate responsibility into the strategic elements of the corporation instead of having a marginalised CSR department with a separate budget, the positive impact on stakeholders can be increased. This raises the question of intentionality – does it count from a moral point of view if your action is not based on a sense of moral duty? This is a philosophical question. Immanuel Kant would say no, but many beneficiaries of corporate responsibility will simply not care.

As mentioned above, in 2011 Porter and Kramer introduced the "big idea" of creating shared value (CSV) – connecting societal and economic progress, for example through reconceiving products and markets and redefining productivity in the value chain (Porter & Kramer, 2011):

> The concept of shared value . . . recognizes that societal needs, not just conventional economic needs, define markets. It also recognizes that social harms or weaknesses frequently create *internal* costs for firms – such as wasted energy or raw materials, costly accidents, and the need for remedial training to compensate for inadequacies in education. And addressing societal harms and constraints does not necessarily raise costs for firms, because they can innovate through using new technologies, operating methods, and management approaches – and as a result, increase their productivity and expand their markets.

There is no doubt that this contribution of Porter and Kramer has been hugely influential in the corporate world (the main audience for the *Harvard Business Review*, in which the article was published), and to some extent also in the academic world. However, many questions have been asked about the originality of the contribution. It is interesting to consider – side by side in Table 3.2 – the views of Porter and Kramer, Friedman and John Ruggie (the former UN Secretary General's Special Representative for Business and Human Rights and main author of the UN Guiding Principles on Business and Human Rights):

Table 3.2 Comparison between the views of Porter and Kramer, Friedman and Ruggie

Porter and Kramer	Friedman	Ruggie
"It is not philanthropy but self-interested behavior to create economic value by creating societal value. If all companies individually pursued shared value connected to their particular businesses, society's overall interests would be served. And companies would acquire legitimacy in the eyes of the communities in which they operated." (Porter & Kramer, 2011: 17)	"It may well be in the long run interest of a corporation that is a major employer in a small community to devote resources to providing amenities to that community or to improving its government." (Friedman, 2002: 36)	"Companies may undertake additional human rights commitments for philanthropic reasons, or to protect and promote their brand, or to develop new business opportunities." (United Nations, 2010: 14)

I have juxtaposed Friedman's quote with Porter and Kramer many times as an exercise with my MBA students (without attribution), and more often than not they struggle to match the authors with the quotes.

A very hard-hitting critique of CSV was published in the *California Management Review* (Crane et al., 2014). In summary, the authors describe the following shortcomings of CSV: "[I]t is unoriginal, it ignores the tensions between social and economic goals, it is naïve about the challenges of business compliance, and it is based on a shallow conception of the role of the corporation in society" (Crane et al., 2014: 131). Ultimately, the authors argue, CSV is "a reactionary rather than transformational response to the crisis of capitalism" (Crane et al., 2014: 131).

They do acknowledge the following strengths of CSV: it appeals to practitioners and scholars, it elevates social goals to a strategic level, it articulates a clear role for governments in responsible behaviour and it adds rigour to the concept of "conscious capitalism" (Crane et al., 2014: 132).

In their response to Crane et al's article, Porter and Kramer state that they find it puzzling that the authors can acknowledge the wide and positive reception of the article, yet claim that it does not say anything new. They find this puzzling,

> especially given the substantial changes in behaviour in corporations around the world, both large and small, that have come as a direct result of the article. Clearly something about this article has moved companies to embrace the idea and act in ways that previous literature has not.
>
> (Porter & Kramer, 2014: 149)

It is hard to believe that Porter and Kramer can make the error of logic of equating the "wide and positive reception" of the article with the novelty of the content. It is almost akin to stating that E.L. James must be a good author because *Fifty Shades of Grey* sold more than a 100 million copies worldwide. Applying the same logic, surely James's book has also moved people to act in ways that previous literature has not.

Porter and Kramer respond briefly to some of the criticism in the article, using the defence that the *Harvard Business Review* does not allow footnotes and countering with the words "mistaken" and "utterly misses our point". Then the gloves come off:

> It is precisely the wishful thinking of writers like Mr. Crane that has led to so many corporate responsibility and sustainability arguments falling on deaf corporate ears, by insisting that profit-seeing (sic) enterprises need to abandon their core purpose for the sake of the greater good.
>
> (Porter & Kramer, 2014: 150)

In their response, Crane and his co-authors accuse Porter and Kramer of presenting a "wilful caricature" of their "fairly nuanced position" and manage to get in the final stab: "Where the wishful thinking really comes in though is in Porter and Kramer's naïve belief that the role of business in addressing the world's major social problems can, or should, only be addressed through the lens of corporate self-interest" (Crane et al., 2014: 152).

Other scholars have also weighed in on this issue. Waddock (2013: 43) places an emphasis on the limitations of the business case:

> As business leaders tackle sustainability, one thing is important to understand: not every action that needs to be taken to create a more sustainable world has what is commonly called a "business case". Some things simply need to be done as part of a precautionary approach, or because they are the right thing to do.

Of course, both sides have a point. It is impossible to deny the "Porter effect", even if one does not like it. Anything with Porter's name attached to it is bound to have a more immediate impact in the corporate world. Secondly, Porter does manage to address a corporate audience in non-academic language, which is essential if one wants to achieve traction and initiate action in the corporate world. Zollo and Mele (2013) put this eloquently. After having acknowledged that "Porter and Kramer's claim to novelty might be relatively weak", they go on to state the following:

> the fact that they could achieve with that one article what scores of academics failed to achieve in the course of decades of work goes entirely to their merit, and rings painful notes to the capacity of management scholars to influence practice with their research, teaching and collective "voice" in the core debates in our society.
>
> (Zollo & Mele, 2013: 19–20)

Georg Kell, former executive director of the UN Global Compact, also welcomed the contribution in very pragmatic terms (Kell, 2013):

> I am personally very delighted that Porter came out with this work because it had an impact on the US where the silly ideological debate between shareholder and stakeholder dominated the public domain. And the shared value notion helped to overcome this and put it in the right direction. . . . And if it takes a Harvard professor to mainstream the concept – great! But it is certainly not new. But it is most welcome.

At the same time, the critique of Crane et al. (2014) is valid. However, a corporate audience does not always concern itself with purported lack of originality, and CEOs do not read footnotes. From a purely pragmatic point of view, if it is Porter's CSV that can get them to do certain things rather than strategic CSR, does it really matter?

There *is* a part that matters. The lack of a normative foundation in CSV brings one back to the business case versus the moral case debate. The "enlightened self-interest" approach is a problematic one because it only works up to a point.

There is always the realisation that from time to time a corporation has to make decisions that will conflict with either its own self-interest or those of its stakeholders. It is easy to justify why bribery is wrong (even if you win the contract, you might go to jail) or why it is good to invest huge amounts of money in environmental technology not required by law (it will improve reputation, and ultimately you will save money). It is not so easy if you have to decide whether to retrench employees, close plants or pay wages that do not conform to trade union demands.

This point is articulated eloquently by Crane et al. (2014: 136) in their critique of CSV: "While seeking win-win opportunities is clearly important, this does not provide guidance for the many situations where social and economic outcomes will not be aligned for all stakeholders."[4]

Kaptein and Wempe (2002) also grapple with this issue. They refer to the "field of tension between the corporate interest, the general interest, and the interests of individual stakeholders" (Kaptein & Wempe, 2002: 2).

This question will be raised again in Chapter 7, when the regulation of corporate responsibility is discussed. It also relates to what Button (2008: 16) calls "the paradox of civic virtue for liberal political societies". Essentially, he asks whether a liberal society can expect the state and its institutions to promote and enforce the values that make the existence of society possible, while at the same time one of the values would be to limit the coercive powers of government.[5]

There seems to be a perceived correlation between the moral case and philanthropy, and between the business case and strategic CSR. However, there is a need to decouple the *motivation* for specific behaviour from the behaviour itself. It is becoming increasingly clear that the most effective way for corporations to respond to societal expectations is to integrate these activities into their day-to-day activities and not to manage these as something separate or peripheral. But doing it in a particular way has nothing to do with the motivation for doing it in the first place.

---

4 For additional commentary on the moral case versus the business case, see Malan (2013).
5 This relates to the response by Donaldson and Dunfee (2000b: 484) to accusations that their theory of Integrative Social Contracts Theory (ISCT), which will be discussed extensively later, is coercively democratic because it makes submission to "majoritarian moral consensus" obligatory.

Power and responsibility

It is important, before proceeding, to investigate the concept of responsibility. Consider the following statements about the well-known case of BP and the 2010 Deepwater Horizon oil spill in the Gulf of Mexico:

- BP was responsible for the oil spill.
- The responsible reaction would have been to communicate honestly to all BP's stakeholders from the very beginning.
- BP's response to accusations of irresponsible behaviour was inadequate.
- Tony Howard, as the CEO of BP, had to take ultimate responsibility for the oil spill.

These statements illustrate the different uses of the word "responsibility". Goodpaster and Matthews (1982: 133) highlight three different meanings of responsibility: to indicate that someone is to blame (you caused this mess, you are responsible), to indicate that something has to be done (you will be the one responsible to fix this) and finally to indicate that some form of trustworthiness can be expected (I trust you, I know you are responsible). It is in this last sense that the moral responsibilities of corporations are addressed, and also where the link between individual actions and corporate actions are clearly illustrated. Responding to Ladd's position quoted earlier, Goodpaster and Matthews (1982: 133) clearly state: "The language of ethics does have a place in the vocabulary of an organization. . . . Organizational agents such as corporations should be no more and no less morally responsible (rational, self-interested, altruistic) than ordinary persons."

Goodpaster and Matthews (1982: 135) argue further that corporations that monitor practices such as employment, health and safety and environmental performance show the same rationality and respect that morally responsible individuals do. We can therefore attribute actions, strategies and also moral responsibilities to corporations just as we can to individuals. Goodpaster and Matthews (1982: 136) illustrate this point with a series of examples that remain as relevant today as they were when they were written in the early 1980s: "Whether the issue be the health effects of sugared cereal or cigarettes, the safety of tires or tampons, civil liberties in the corporation or the community, an organization reveals its character as surely as a person does."

The position of Goodpaster and Matthews (1982), that an organisation reveals its character in the same way that an individual does, provides a common sense approach to business ethics and corporate responsibility that remains attractive today to practitioners and lawmakers, that is, those who do not necessarily have an interest in a theoretical grounding of moral responsibility. It is this approach, as well as the experiences – both good and bad, but particularly the bad, of the impact that corporations can have on society – that has resulted in what Williams refers to as the growing consensus about the moral obligations and the emerging new role for the corporation in society (Williams, 2008: 435). This view is also in line with the previously mentioned division of individual and corporate levels of business ethics that is often used in discussions about business ethics (together with industry and systemic levels). The individual and company levels are intertwined with each other, with collective individual behaviour (especially facilitated by leadership) determining the ethical behaviour at the corporate level.

According to Enderle (2006: 111), responsibility involves three components: firstly, the subject of responsibility (who is responsible?); secondly, the content of responsibility (for what is one responsible?); and, thirdly, the authority of responsibility (to whom is one responsible?).

Kaptein and Wempe (2002) distinguish between amoral, functional and autonomy models. While the amoral model does not acknowledge corporate moral responsibility as a meaningful concept (in line with Friedman's views), the functional model acknowledges an "organised character of actions", but this is reduced to the individual responsibility of employees. They argue in favour of the autonomy model in terms of which the "corporation can be conceived as an independent moral unit" (Kaptein & Wempe, 2002: 107) or a social entity "separate from the individuals who represent the company" (Kaptein & Wempe, 2002: 110). They discuss a number of different variations of the autonomy model. This includes the projection approach of Goodpaster and Matthews (because there are similarities between corporations and individuals we can project moral autonomy onto the corporation) and the secondary moral actor theory of Werhane and Spit (because management comprises moral players, the corporation can be judged as a secondary moral actor). Kaptein and Wempe (2002: 125) propose an integrated corporate moral practices theory: "Corporations are moral entities because they consist of independent practices that can be subjected to moral evaluation." This is also in line with the position of Enderle (2014: 172) who argues that corporations can be held morally responsible for their acts because, as collective entities, they act with intention. This view is also supported by the generally accepted legal position that corporations are persons and that therefore they have both rights and responsibilities. The famous United States Supreme Court case from 1886 (*Santa Clara County versus Southern Pacific Railroad Company*[6]) is often used as an example in this regard, where the judge declared that corporations are persons and therefore entitled to the same constitutional protection as persons. More recently, judgements in a few cases in the United States reconfirmed this position. In 2010, it was ruled in *Citizens United versus Federal Election Commission*[7] that the government could not restrict political

6 https://supreme.justia.com/cases/federal/us/118/394/, accessed 15 September 2015.
7 www.law.cornell.edu/supct/html/08-205.ZS.html, accessed 15 September 2015.

spending by corporations, and in 2014 it was ruled in *Burwell, Secretary of Health and Human Services versus Hobby Lobby Stores*[8] that a corporation could choose not to make contraception available to its employees due to religious objections.

Hsieh has examined the question about the responsibility of multinational corporations to provide aid to persons in developing countries – this is specifically relevant with regards to discussions about the UN Global Compact and the Sustainable Development Goals, because so many signatories to the UN Global Compact are multinational corporations with operations in developing economies. Hsieh (2009b: 100) uses the Rawlsian concept of justice to argue why such a responsibility might exist in some cases. Drawing on Rawls's distinction between obligations (arising from voluntary acts) and natural duties (these apply regardless of voluntary acts and the most important one according to Rawls is to support and further just institutions), Hsieh (2009b: 101) illustrates how this natural duty grounds the responsibility of business organisations to provide assistance, to help bring about conditions of justice in countries where these conditions do not exist and to make a contribution to reform legal and political institutions.

In an earlier contribution, Hsieh (2004) discusses the duty of assistance within the context of the principles of the UN Global Compact. Using the same argument of Rawlsian justice, he argues that there are conditions under which multinational corporations (he calls them transnational corporations) have obligations to fulfil a "limited duty of assistance" toward those living in developing economies (Hsieh, 2004: 643). Hsieh is particularly interested in positive obligations. He argues that there is common agreement that corporations should not engage in harmful activities. However, this is not so clear for positive obligations, for example to provide certain benefits and services in developing countries, especially when those benefits and services are commonly believed to be the responsibilities of governments. He uses the language employed by Rawls in *The Law of Peoples*, by referring to well-ordered societies and burdened societies. Well-ordered societies are described as non-aggressive, with secure human rights for all members, a system of law that can impose duties and obligations, and where those who administer the legal system understand the law to be guided by a common good idea of justice (Hsieh, 2004: 646). Burdened societies are described by Rawls, quoted by Hsieh, as those whose "historical, social and economic circumstances make their achieving a well-ordered regime, whether liberal or decent, difficult if not impossible" (Hsieh, 2004: 646). Under these circumstances, according to Rawls, well-ordered societies have a duty of assistance to burdened societies.

---

8 www.huffingtonpost.com/adam-winkler/corporations-are-people-a_b_5543833.html, accessed 15 September 2015.

Hsieh would like to find out whether this duty of assistance can be extended to multinational corporations. Using the UN Global Compact principles (nine at the time of his writing[9]), he argues that the UN Global Compact attributes obligations to corporations, similar to what Rawls attributed to governments. To give content to these obligations, Hsieh introduces three principles: the principle of assistance, the principle of limited scope and the principle of accountability.

According to the principle of assistance, where corporations benefit directly from the burdensome conditions in which they operate, they have a duty of assistance (Hsieh, 2004: 650). According to the principle of limited scope, they cannot be expected to contribute more than the amount by which they directly benefit (Hsieh, 2004: 651). According to the principle of accountability, corporations are obliged to assist with mechanisms through which those affected by their activities can contest corporate decisions (Hsieh, 2004: 658).

Hsieh (2009b) responds to the issue of assistance from another angle. He discusses Dunfee's view that managers are morally permitted, and even at times required, to use corporate resources to alleviate human misery, even if this comes at the expense of shareholders. This question is relevant because quite often there is a tension between the intuition that such assistance would be the right thing to do, and acknowledging at the same time that shareholders have a special claim over corporate resources. Hsieh quotes Scanlon, who formulated the Rescue Principle:

> [I]f you are presented with a situation in which you can prevent something very bad from happening, or alleviate someone's dire plight, by making only a slight (or even moderate) sacrifice, then it would be wrong not to do so.
>
> (Hsieh, 2009b: 556)

Dunfee's argument is contained in four guiding principles (Hsieh, 2009b: 555):

- There is a presumption that all corporate actions must be aimed at maximising shareholder wealth.
- Managers must respond to and anticipate existing and changing marketplace morality that might have a negative impact on shareholder wealth.
- The presumption in principle one can be rebutted if clear and convincing evidence exists that the marketplace morality relevant to the firm would justify a decision which will not maximise shareholder wealth directly.
- Managers must act consistently with universal norms (Dunfee uses the term "hypernorms" which will be discussed as part of ISCT).

---

9   The 10th principle on anti-corruption was only added at a later stage due to extensive lobbying.

Hsieh distinguishes this approach from stakeholder theory and corporate citizenship theory, because of the prominence that is still given to the shareholders (Hsieh, 2009a: 559):

> Shareholder interests are not simply accorded more weight relative to the interests of other parties. Rather, their interests are best understood as carrying a kind of lexical priority that can be overridden by the interests of other parties only in specific circumstances, e.g., the need for rescue in the face of a catastrophe.

One of the reasons why there is substantial conceptual confusion in this area is because the fields of business ethics and corporate responsibility are not only multidisciplinary but also straddle the divide between theory and practice. In his review of *Ties That Bind* by Donaldson and Dunfee (1999), John Boatright (2000: 452) makes this point rather eloquently: "How can any theory of ethics that is rigorous enough to pass muster with picky philosophers possibly give guidance to busy, hardheaded business managers?" Yet this remains one of the most productive challenges on both sides – for academics to present their thinking in more accessible ways, and for business managers and executives to understand that there must be more substance to their strategies than spreadsheets and PowerPoint presentations.

To conclude this section, the position that corporations have moral responsibilities is restated. At the very least, this is supported by a growing consensus within all sectors of society, including the business community itself. Although it is important to distinguish conceptually between moral and social responsibility, the way in which moral responsibility applies within a corporate environment is intrinsically linked to social responsibilities, because corporations are part of the society within which they exist.

If there is agreement on the existence of these moral responsibilities and their basic social application, this does not necessarily help people to understand where they come from. This is the focus of normative theory and will be discussed next.

Purpose and value: a theoretical overview

Questions about purpose are situated within the field of normative theory. Value is a more elusive concept because it is sometimes, but not always, used in a normative context. We therefore start with a brief discussion of normative theory and follow one of many lines that includes an overview of social contract theory and stakeholder theory. Extensive attention is given to the work of Tom Donaldson. Donaldson has been one of the most influential figures in the field of business ethics. Integrative Social Contracts Theory, developed with the late Tom Dunfee more than 20 years ago, still has huge relevance for the world of business, especially multinational corporations. Building on this earlier work, Donaldson and Walsh (2015) propose a theory of business that defines the purpose of business, and the chapter will conclude with a brief discussion of these ideas.

Normative theory

Normative theory is concerned with ethical behaviour and the distinction between right and wrong. Parfit (2011: 150) discusses the "ordinary" sense of the word "wrong", used in a moral way as opposed to the non-moral use, for example when someone gives the wrong answer to a question. According to him the "ordinary" sense of wrong is most plausible when we consider the acts of people who know all the morally relevant facts, but he then makes an additional distinction between wrong in the fact-relative sense (when something would be wrong if we knew all the morally relevant facts), the belief-relative sense (when something would be wrong if our beliefs about the facts were true) and wrong in the evidence-relative sense (if we believed, correctly, that the available evidence gives us decisive reasons to believe something would be wrong) (Parfit, 2011: 151).

In normative theory a distinction is made between descriptive ethics (describing something as it is, for example an attitude or behaviour), and prescriptive ethics (prescribing how something ought to be). Different normative theories use different methodologies and can often come up with different solutions to the same ethical problem. The naturalistic fallacy is the logical mistake of deducing an ethical conclusion from empirical research (the move from an "is" to an "ought"). Simply because something *is* the way it is does not mean that therefore it *ought* to be the way it is. Ethical positions must be justified, based on a specific theory. Donaldson discusses the "open question argument" which was framed by the philosopher G.E. Moore in the early twentieth century. According to this argument, any state of affairs in the world is logically subject to the open question: "Is it good?" (Donaldson, 2012: 259).

Three of the most popular and well-known normative theories are consequentialism, where ethical decisions are made based on an assessment of the likely consequences of an action; deontology, where decisions are made based on rights and duties; and virtue ethics, where the focus is not on assessing the action, but rather the individual involved. The two theoretical approaches that have been selected for discussion here are social contract theory and stakeholder theory, which are both part of the deontological tradition. Using the language of rights and duties, these theories provide practical frameworks that corporations can apply to align their behaviour with their perceived responsibilities. It is argued that the solutions that they offer are more durable than the quick-fix solutions provided by a consequentialist cost-benefit calculation.

This is a preference that will not be defended at length, but hopefully the explanations that follow will be convincing.[10]

Although the purpose here is not a detailed philosophical discussion, it is useful to spend a little time looking at the concept of natural law. Laws of nature are described as "universal, eternal, and independent of the will of any human legislator. They are discovered by reason and are the basis of natural rights and duties" (Bunnin & Yu, 2004: 380). There are two major forms of natural law theory: classical and modern. According to Bunnin and Yu (2004: 456), the classical theory is based on the distinction between nature and convention and draws a direct line between natural law and justice. Natural law can be grounded either in religion or human nature but is always discovered by human reason.[11] The concept of law is used because the theory refers to the "standards of right choosing, standards which are normative, that is rationally directive and 'obligatory', because they are true and choice otherwise than in accordance with them is unreasonable" (Craig, 1998: 685).

Modern natural law theory "claims that natural law grants natural rights to each individual" (Bunnin & Yu, 2004:). According to this approach, political rights and obligations are derived through a social contract. The contributions of Locke, Rousseau and Rawls are based on this approach and discussed in more detail below.

Social contract theory

Social contract theory postulates that universal rules can be agreed upon by human beings, more specifically between individuals and the state. A hypothetical social contract allows individuals to progress from the state of nature that Thomas Hobbes described – more or less at the same time that *The Threatened Swan* was painted – as "solitary, poor, nasty, brutish and short", but also

---

10 For a more detailed discussion of these theoretical approaches and their application within a business environment, see Kaptein and Wempe (2002: 54–80), and Smith (2009: 5–8).

11 It falls outside the scope of this study to provide a detailed assessment of natural law, but it is important to note that the concept has been challenged on both legal and philosophical grounds. Consider the following view from Oliver Wendell Holmes, the American jurist who famously described the United States Constitution as "an experiment, as all life is an experiment" (http://en.wikipedia.org/wiki/Oliver_Wendell_Holmes,_Jr., accessed 18 October 2010). Holmes was a moral sceptic and fundamentally opposed to natural law: "There is in all men a demand for the superlative, so much so that the poor devil who has no other way of reaching it attains it by getting drunk. It seems to me that this demand is at the bottom of the philosopher's effort to prove that truth is absolute and of the jurist's search for criteria of universal validity which he collects under the head of natural law."

implies that individuals have to comply with the terms of the contract that they agree to. Other than Hobbes, political philosophers who wrote extensively on this topic include John Locke, Jean-Jacques Rousseau and John Rawls.

The basic principle of a social contract is present in Hobbes's discussion of natural law. Hobbes (Newton, 2004: 99) defines natural law as a "general rule, found out by reason, by which a man is forbidden to do that which is destructive of his life". According to Hobbes, the first law of nature is "to seek peace and to follow it". The second law is defined as follows by Hobbes, quoted in Newton:

> that a man be willing, when others are so too, as far forth as for peace and defense of himself he shall think it necessary, to lay down this right to all things; and be contented with so much liberty against other men as he would allow other men against himself.
>
> (Newton, 2004: 99)

Present in this formulation is Hobbes's view that human beings should submit themselves to the Leviathan to obtain peace. It is also the precursor to Kant's categorical imperative.

John Locke defined natural law as follows:

> [T]he state of Nature has a law of Nature to govern it, which obliges every one, and reason, which is that law, teaches all mankind who will but consult it, that being all equal and independent, no one ought to harm another in his life, health, liberty or possessions.
>
> (Newton, 2004: 102)

Within Locke's writing there is an emphasis on the protection of property (as well as the more abstract notions of life and liberty) – this is regulated by the social contract and the law in general.

In the work of Jean-Jacques Rousseau a shift takes place in the concept of the social contract from a focus on nature to one of convention. This is in line with a more individualistic view of humanity and therefore moves closer to the idea that all people need to participate in the construction of, rather than simply discover, the rules of society: "[T]he social order is a sacred right which serves as a basis for all others. Yet this right does not come from nature; it is therefore based on conventions" (Newton, 2004: 111).

John Rawls advances the discussion about the social contract by introducing the veil of ignorance, a concept that increases the fairness of the contract itself. Under the veil of ignorance, individuals select basic principles that will form the groundwork of all other agreements – these are the basic principles of justice that Rawls calls "justice as fairness". The veil of ignorance is introduced to "[leave] aside those aspects of the social world that seem arbitrary from a moral point of view" (Rawls, 2001: 55). These aspects include natural endowment or social circumstance (Rawls, 2001: 55):

> Somehow we must nullify the effects of specific contingencies which put men at odds and tempt them to exploit social and natural circumstances to their own advantage. Now in order to do this I assume that the parties are situated behind a veil of ignorance. They do not know how the various alternatives will affect their own particular case and they are obliged to evaluate principles solely on the basis of general considerations.

Rawls (2001: 56) suggests that – under these conditions – the following basic principles will be agreed upon:

- First: each person is to have an equal right to the most extensive basic liberty[12] compatible with a similar liberty for others.
- Second: social and economic inequalities are to be arranged so that they are both (a) reasonably expected to be to everyone's advantage and (b) attached to positions and offices open to all.

In other words, inequality is not incompatible with justice, but fairness dictates that inequality should be arranged in such a way that it is to everyone's advantage. This is very different from the utilitarian argument that will simply look at the sum total of benefits – in the case of social contract theory, inequality in terms of wealth can only be justified if it results in an increase in wealth on both sides of the equation. For example, if I am already wealthy and want to increase the gap between my own wealth and that of the poor, this can only be allowed if my actions will also increase the relative wealth of the poor.

Stakeholder theory

The original social contract is negotiated between a government and its citizens, and it is perhaps understandable that the application of this theory to the business environment might lead some people to believe that the social (business) contract is only between the corporation and its shareholders. This idea does not accord with the view that a corporation has responsibilities,

---

12 According to Rawls (2001) the "basic liberties of citizens are, roughly speaking, political liberty (the right to vote and to be eligible for public office) together with freedom of speech and assembly; liberty of conscience and freedom of thought; freedom of the person along with the right to hold (personal) property; and freedom from arbitrary arrest and seizure as defined by the concept of the rule of law".

including some form of contractual obligation, relating to many other entities other than shareholders. The latter view is embodied in stakeholder theory.

Stakeholders are conventionally defined as those who have an impact and are impacted upon by an organisation's decisions and actions. However, it is interesting to go back to the origin of the use of the word in management theory. In 1963 an internal memorandum at the Stanford Research Institute referred to stakeholders as "those groups without whose support the organisation would cease to exist", thus highlighting the strategic nature of stakeholders.[13] In other words, stakeholders play a critical role in the well-being – and ultimately the survival – of the organisation. Therefore, they cannot be seen as groups that must merely be kept informed through slick marketing and communication campaigns. This view is still held by many organisations that do not understand the strategic nature of stakeholder engagement.

Ed Freeman, considered by many to be the father of stakeholder theory, describes the basic tenets of the approach as follows (Freeman et al., 2010: 24):

> Business can be understood as a set of relationships among groups which have a stake in the activities that make up the business. Business is about how customers, suppliers, employees, financiers . . . communities, and managers interact and create value. To understand a business is to know how these relationships work. And the executive's or entrepreneur's job is to manage and shape these relationships.

Figure 3.3 displays a typical outline of the stakeholders of an organisation, making a distinction between primary and secondary stakeholders.

Stakeholder theory replaces the notion that the managers of corporations have a duty only to shareholders with the idea that there is a broader, fiduciary relationship with stakeholders, "those groups who have a stake in or a claim on the firm" (Freeman, 2002: 39). Of course, even within the confines of shareholder theory there are constraints, because the fiduciary duty of the directors is to the company, not to the shareholders.

Conventionally, the stakeholders in the firm are suppliers, customers, employees, shareholders, local communities and managers themselves. Freeman (2002: 39) argues that "each of these stakeholder groups has a right not to be treated as a means to some end, and therefore must participate in determining the future direction of the firm in which they have a stake".[14]

---

13 www.boundless.com/accounting/textbooks/boundless-accounting-textbook/introduction-to-accounting-1/overview-of-key-elements-of-the-business-19/business-stakeholders-internal-and-external-117-6595/, accessed 21 December 2014.

14 For a brief video clip where Freeman discusses stakeholder theory, view www.youtube.com/watch?v=bIRUaLcvPe8, accessed 23 October 2010.

Figure 3.3 Stakeholder map

Source: Adapted from Freeman et al. (2010: 14)

As suggested by the view that stakeholders have the right not to be treated as a means to an end, there is a strong normative component to stakeholder theory. Freeman (2002: 45) suggests that we need business *and* moral terms to complete sentences like "Corporations ought to be governed . . ." or "Managers ought to act to . . .". He describes stakeholder theory as a "genre of stories about how we could live" (Freeman, 2002: 44), rather than a rigid, prescriptive theory. Attempts to prescribe *one* normative core or *one* stakeholder theory are "at best a disguised attempt to smuggle a normative core past the unsophisticated noses of other unsuspecting academics who are just happy to see the end of the stockholder orthodoxy" (Freeman, 2002: 45). This conscious attempt to steer clear of absolutism will be revisited when Integrative Social Contract Theory (ISCT) is introduced in the next section.

The acknowledgement of different stakeholders in the corporation also sets the scene for different agreements – or social contracts – to be agreed upon between them. Once again, this serves as an introduction to ISCT, which allows for the creation of multiple contracts (the so-called micro contracts). Freeman's discussion of the "Doctrine of Fair Contracts" uses the same "veil of ignorance" thought experiment, in this case applied where individual stakeholders try to agree to the "rules of the game". Freeman (2002: 46–47) argues that stakeholders would agree to the following principles:

- Entry and exit: each stakeholder must be able to determine when an agreement exists and also be able to determine whether it is valid or not.
- Governance: there must be consensus among all stakeholders about how the rules of the game can be changed.
- Externalities: if a contract between two parties imposes a cost on a third party, that party has the right to become a party to the contract, and the terms should be renegotiated.
- Contracting costs: all parties must share the cost of contracting.
- Agency: any agent must serve the interests of all the stakeholders.
- Limited immortality: because the continued existence of the corporation is in the interest of all stakeholders, it should be managed as if it can continue to serve the interests of all stakeholders through time.

It has been mentioned that there is growing consensus about moral obligations and the emerging new role of the corporation in society. But just because there is growing consensus – or even if there were to be complete consensus – does not denote that the consensus position is necessarily acceptable from an ethical perspective. Bridging the gap between the "is" and the "ought" is one of the claims of Donaldson and Dunfee's Integrative Social Contracts Theory. It is time to look at Integrative Social Contracts Theory in more detail. Even though it was introduced more than two decades ago and perhaps did not get the attention it deserved, the fundamentals of this theory provide one of the most solid theoretical foundations for responsible business behaviour.

Integrative Social Contracts Theory

Against the backdrop of the previous discussion about normative theory and more specifically social contract theory and stakeholder theory, this section introduces Integrative Social Contracts Theory (ISCT). This theory was developed by Tom Donaldson and Thomas Dunfee to provide guidance on ethical issues in international business, where conflicts often appear between a global head office and country operations. Companies are faced with the question: do we have one set of rules and principles that will apply everywhere, or do we allow our country operations to do that themselves? The risks of both absolutism and relativism are present in this question, and Donaldson and Dunfee tried to avoid the pitfalls of both.

What follows below is a general introduction to the main tenets of the theory, the links with stakeholder theory, as well as major critiques of the theory. ISCT was introduced more than 20 years ago and has not received the attention it deserves. The work of Donaldson has evolved, culminating in the article in which a theory of business was proposed (Donaldson & Walsh, 2015). His work has suffered the unenviable but somehow inevitable fate of superior theoretical contributions – it lost the race against inferior contributions such as Creating Shared Value (CSV) that offered solutions that seemed less complicated and more attractive.

But without arguing for a return to this work, it is very important to revisit and see what we can still learn from these important contributions and then apply that within the current theoretical context.

One of the major strengths of the work of Donaldson and Dunfee is that they provide a practical framework for decision-making that is based on sound theory, without getting stuck in the meta-debate about whether there can be one all-encompassing approach to ethics. They claim that it does not matter which normative theory is relevant for the decision-maker: "ISCT counsels economic practitioners to attend specifically to the reality of microsocial contracts" (Donaldson & Dunfee, 2000: 482).

In his earlier work, Donaldson (1989) argues that morality should be applied to international affairs and – more specifically – international business. According to him this is the case whether morality is simply defined as enlightened self-interest or something more fundamental. He provides a detailed discussion of both cultural relativism and Hobbesianism and illustrates how both these approaches fail to argue convincingly against the application of morality. In an article written by Donaldson in 1996, the basic outline of ISCT is already present; in it he proposes that companies must be guided by three principles: "Respect for core human values, which determine the absolute moral threshold for all business activities; [r]espect for local traditions; and [t]he belief that context matters when deciding what is right and what is wrong" (Donaldson, 2001: 478).

The core human values (later referred to as hypernorms) to which Donaldson refers are defined as respect for human dignity, respect for basic rights and good citizenship (Donaldson, 2001: 479). Because these values are too vague to provide specific guidance, there is a requirement for companies to develop more specific codes: "Whenever intolerable business situations arise, managers should be guided by precise statements that spell out the behaviour and operating practices that the company demands" (Donaldson, 2001: 480). The development and implementation of effective internal codes remains one of the single biggest challenges for corporations around the world. In broad terms there been two main approaches: a compliance-based approach that provides detailed information and is usually more focused on the prevention of unethical behaviour, and a values-based approach that encourages ethical behaviour and allows employees to take a specific context into account when they make decisions. Both of these could be viewed as micro contracts in the language of ISCT.

Summary of Integrative Social Contracts Theory

In a nutshell, ISCT suggests that there is a universally binding moral threshold (comprising universal principles or hypernorms) that would apply anywhere in the world. At the same time, context matters from a practical as well as theoretical perspective when deciding between right and wrong. According to the theory, corporations should have respect for local customs and conventions and can therefore negotiate micro contracts within an area called moral free space, as long as they do not transgress the universal moral threshold. Moral free space displays similarities with the more familiar grey areas of ethical decision-making, although all agreements made within this space have ethical standing.

Moral free space is defined as "[t]he freedom of individuals to form or join communities and to act jointly to establish moral rules applicable to the members of the community" (Donaldson & Dunfee, 1999: 38). If a norm or a moral rule is generated within moral free space and has the support of the majority of the community, it is said to be "authentic". A community is defined as "a self-defined, self-circumscribed group of people who interact in the context of shared tasks, values, or goals and who are capable of establishing norms of ethical behavior for themselves" (Donaldson & Dunfee, 1999: 39).

The links with natural law (universal values compared to hypernorms) and stakeholder theory (through an emphasis on local context and local communities) are immediately evident.

As illustrated in Figure 3.4, ISCT provides a sound, normative framework for global business through the concept of hypernorms. According to Dunfee (2006: 304), the primary purpose of ISCT is "to provide a means of practical guidance to ethical decision makers, particularly managers". At the same time the introduction of moral free space provides the opportunity for meaningful local action, the ultimate way in which the success of initiatives such as the UN Global Compact should be measured.

When they introduced their theory formally, Donaldson and Dunfee (1994) positioned ISCT as an attempt to bridge the gap between empirical and normative research in business ethics, where researchers with philosophical training mainly employ normative, non-empirical methods, while researchers in business and management science with training in empirical methods apply their techniques – mostly in descriptive fashion – to areas such as managerial motivation and investigating the relationship between ethical behaviour and financial performance. Donaldson and Dunfee (1994: 254) describe their proposed theory as a "normative theory . . . which incorporates empirical findings as part of the contractarian process of making normative judgments".

The basic message of ISCT is that "implicit agreements constitute part of the basic software of business ethics" (Donaldson & Dunfee, 2000a: 437). As opposed to conventional social contract theory that investigates the contracts between citizens and governments, ISCT focuses on how economic participants will define business ethics.

Figure 3.4 Visual representation of ISCT

The concept of a "veil of ignorance" is important in this regard. Rawls introduced the concept in order to ensure objective decision-making. He explains it as follows (Rawls, 1971: 12):

> It is understood as a purely hypothetical situation characterized so as to lead to a certain conception of justice. Among the essential features of this situation is that no one knows his place in society, his class position or social status, nor does any one know his fortune in the distribution of natural assets and abilities, his intelligence, strength, and the like. I shall even assume that the parties do not know their conceptions of the good or their special psychological propensities. The principles of justice are chosen behind a veil of ignorance. This ensures that no one is advantaged or disadvantaged in the choice of principles by the outcome of natural chance or the contingency of social circumstances.

The veil of ignorance in ISCT is more revealing than the one suggested by Rawls. The basic assumption made by Donaldson and Dunfee in their thought experiment conducted to come up with ISCT is that participants do not know their economic standing, for example which company they work for, nor what their personal wealth is. However, they are granted knowledge about their economic and political preferences as well as a basic sense of right and wrong. Under these circumstances, participants are then hypothetically gathered for "a global congress to construct an agreement that would provide a fundamental framework for ethical behaviour in economic activities" (Donaldson & Dunfee, 2000: 438). In fact, in their early introduction of the theory the authors do not use the concept of a veil of ignorance to describe their thought experiment, because they deem the requirement for consensus to be sufficient (Donaldson & Dunfee, 1994: 260):

> The principles that people would choose behind such a veil of ignorance are in this way presumed to be fair. . . . In other instances of social-contract reasoning, fairness is secured simply by including among the contractors all persons whose interests are affected and by requiring consensus in the adoption of the terms of the contract – without the additional device of a veil of ignorance. It is the second strategy that we adopt.

In this formulation one can already see the authors' affinity for a stakeholder approach. The use of the word "integrative" emphasises that

> ISCT is based upon a hypothetical social contract whose terms allow for the generation of binding ethical obligations through the recognition of actual norms created in real social and economic communities. A hypothetical social contract is thereby integrated with real or extant social contracts.
>
> (Dunfee, 2006: 304)

Again, one can see the link between the theoretical (the macro contract of the fundamental framework is hypothetical) and the empirical (*real* micro contracts within *real* communities that can be studied empirically).

According to the authors, the following core assumptions will frame discussions about such a framework:

- Good answers to moral problems require an acquaintance with community-specific norms – knowledge about theory alone is not good enough. This is referred to as "bounded moral rationality" (Donaldson & Dunfee, 1999: 28). The authors use the example of corporate downsizing and illustrate how complex circumstances will prevent a simple application of any chosen moral theory: "[R]easonable individuals armed with the same facts and who accept the same ethical theory may achieve different results in applying the theory" (Donaldson & Dunfee, 1999: 29).
- High-quality and more efficient economic interaction is preferred to lower quality and less efficiency, and ethical behaviour can enhance both the quality and efficiency of such interaction. By way of example, high

levels of trust within a society will reduce transaction costs because of the reduced need for expensive administrative and legal procedures.

- "Ceteris paribus, economic activity that is consistent with the cultural, philosophical, or religious attitudes of economic actors is preferable to economic activity that is not" (Donaldson & Dunfee, 1999: 28). The impact of these attitudes on economic activity and ultimately also on ethical decision making is referred to as a discretionary area, or "moral free space".

Based on these assumptions, Donaldson and Dunfee argue that their hypothetical global congress for business ethics will not be able to agree on a detailed set of ethical rules and guidelines, but rather will agree on a process or broad framework. This framework of business ethics is what they call the Global ISCT Macrosocial Contract for Economic Ethics. The terms of the contract are the following (Donaldson & Dunfee, 1999: 46):

(1) Local economic communities must have moral free space in which they may generate ethical norms for their members through microsocial contracts. (2) Norm-generating microsocial contracts must be grounded in consent, buttressed by the rights of individual members to exercise voice[15] and exit. (3) In order to become obligatory (legitimate), a microsocial contract norm must be compatible with hypernorms. (4) In cases of conflict between norms satisfying macrosocial contract terms 1 to 3, priority must be established through the application of rules consistent with the spirit and letter of the macrosocial contract.

Members of a particular community have an ethical obligation to abide by the existing authentic norms, as long as these norms do not violate hypernorms. Hypernorms are defined as "principles so fundamental that they constitute norms by which all others are to be judged", and are "discernible in a convergence of religious, political and philosophical thought" (Donaldson & Dunfee, 2000: 441). There are three distinct hypernorm categories (Donaldson & Dunfee, 1999: 53):

- Procedural hypernorms – these stipulate the rights of voice and exit, and are defined as the conditions "essential to support consent in microsocial contracts".
- Structural hypernorms – principles "that establish and support essential background institutions in society"; these are necessary for political and social organisation.
- Substantive hypernorms – these are the fundamental "concepts of the right and the good".

---

15 The right of voice is defined as "the right of members of a community to speak out for or against existing and developing norms" (Donaldson & Dunfee, 1999: 43).

Whether hypernorms have their origin in natural law or elsewhere does not concern Donaldson and Dunfee very much:

> [w]hatever the final answer to the question of whether hypernorms have sources in nature as immutable verities, or instead reflect the common humanity of global citizens as similar solutions are found to shared problems across the world, that answer is not critical to their value within ISCT.
>
> (Donaldson & Dunfee, 1999: 52)

Donaldson and Dunfee (1999: 60) include the following types of evidence in support of hypernorms – the applicability of two or more of the points below per hypernorm would be sufficient for a "rebuttable presumption that it constitutes a hypernorm":

- Widespread consensus that a principle is universal.
- Inclusion in well-known global industry standards.
- Supported by prominent NGOs, regional government organisations, global business organisations or an international community of professionals.
- Consistently referred to as a global ethical standard by the international media.
- Consistent with precepts of major religions and philosophies, as well as findings concerning universal human values.
- Supported by the laws of many different countries.

If an authentic norm violates a hypernorm it is not a legitimate norm.[16] A member of a community would be within his or her rights to deny the legitimacy of an authentic norm in such a case. Donaldson and Dunfee are not specific about whether members would be morally obliged to oppose offending norms, but they do acknowledge the right to civil disobedience. Even if norms are both authentic and legitimate, this does not mean that each member of the community has to agree with them (although they would have to abide by them). Members have the right of voice (to speak up) or exit (to leave). Both of these, especially the right to exit, can come at a high price, and this is acknowledged by Donaldson and Dunfee (1999: 42).

Integrative Social Contracts Theory and stakeholder theory

Even though Donaldson and Dunfee make a distinction between their definition of community and the concept of stakeholders, it is argued by them that the concepts are sufficiently similar for ISCT to be interpreted as entirely

---

16 An authentic norm is generated within moral free space and has the support of the majority of the community.

compatible with stakeholder theory. They do acknowledge that the concept of a stakeholder is useful in terms of identifying relevant ISCT communities (Donaldson & Dunfee, 2000: 441), and Dunfee talks about the promising recommendation of coupling ISCT with stakeholder dialogue. Dunfee (2006: 314) describes the relationship between ISCT and stakeholder concepts as follows:

> By emphasizing relevant communities, ISCT is broadly supportive of the key idea of stakeholder management: that the interests of those who are affected by or are at risk as a result of business decisions should be considered. That is not to say that ISCT is co-extensive with stakeholder management. The focus of ISCT is on communities and norms, not on individual stakeholders and interests not reflected in community norms. It may well be that the decision-maker community may follow a norm of stakeholder management, in which case, the overlap between stakeholder ideas and ISCT would be nearly perfect. But such an outcome requires the existence and identification of a "stakeholder" norm within a relevant, priority community.

He acknowledges that stakeholder dialogue can provide a "more fine-grained test of authenticity" at the microsocial level, and also that it can be "part of the glue that holds together the assent essential at the community level" (Dunfee, 2006: 321). Dunfee provides a sober assessment of the relationship between the two (Dunfee, 2006: 321):

> Although in one sense stakeholder concepts and ISCT can be seen as competing for the attention of moral theorists, in a more basic sense they can be seen as complementary. The rich literature on identification of stakeholders points the way toward recognition of ISCT-relevant communities. ISCT, in turn, provides a compatible normative basis for sorting among competing stakeholder claims and solving other thorny issues confronting stakeholder approaches.

Freeman et al. (2010: 219) briefly discuss ISCT and call it "a powerful tool for thinking about the moral sub-structure of economic life". Their discussion is mostly descriptive, and they do not express their own opinion on the relationship between ISCT and stakeholder theory.

Major critiques of Integrative Social Contracts Theory

Dunfee (2006) defines recurring themes in literature critical of ISCT, including questions about the nature, value and existence of hypernorms, questions about the practicality of ISCT as a decision-making tool and questions about the sufficiency of justifications for creating ethical obligations for managers. In addition, some critics have called for a full-fledged moral theory to back up ISCT.

HYPERNORMS

The recurring critiques concerning hypernorms address the following questions (Dunfee, 2006: 305):

- Can hypernorms be identified for actual decision-making?
- Are hypernorms sufficiently justified in the ISCT macrosocial contract?
- Should hypernorms be significantly redefined, or are they even necessary to the overall ISCT framework?
- Do hypernorms change or evolve over time?

In terms of the link between hypernorms and actual decision-making, the point is made that the hypernorms really form part of the thought experiment to construct the macro contract and should not be too detailed:

> the more specific and detailed an alleged substantive hypernorm is, the more likely it will be controversial, with many disputing its existence. . . . If Moses had come down from the mountain with 128 000 commandments, their credibility and impact would have been greatly reduced.
>
> (Dunfee, 2006: 307)

Dunfee (2006: 308) also discusses the work of Soule, who argued that detailed qualifications to hypernorms will make them irrelevant in the event of rapidly changing circumstances.

With regard to the justification of hypernorms, specifically substantive hypernorms, critics like Boatright and Van Oosterhout are concerned about the *source*. They would like to see some external ethical theory that would serve as the foundation of hypernorms. They briefly discuss the suggestion by Van Oosterhout that the commitments implicit in a contractualist framework (individualism, freedom, etc.) can provide this foundation.

With regard to the view that hypernorms are not required for ISCT to be effective (Frederick referred to their use as a "philosophistic fallacy"), Dunfee (2006: 31) states the following: "hypernorms are an important bulwark against cultural relativism. If they are removed, leaving only authentic norms and the moral free space component of ISCT, then some other means of guarding against relativism is required."

On the question of whether hypernorms can change over time, Dunfee (2006: 311) keeps an open mind. He argues that this would depend on an understanding of the basic nature of hypernorms:

> If they were assumed to be immutable prescriptions from the natural law, as some would believe, then they would not be considered changeable . . . if substantive hypernorms were assumed to reflect the wisdom and experience of humanity across time and circumstance, then they would be assumed to change on the basis of new wisdom and context.

DECISION-MAKING

Many people regard ISCT as too complex, and Dunfee has to agree that a four-page decision tree (Donaldson & Dunfee, 1999: 208–211) for applying ISCT does not ease the process. He also acknowledges that a manager who faces an urgent predicament cannot be expected to conduct research into the attitudes and behaviours of community members before making an ethical decision (Dunfee, 2006: 313). However, the long list of applications that have already taken place, which include diverse issues such as conflicting cross-cultural norms, downsizing, computer ethics, bribery, direct marketing, consumer privacy, sweatshop labour standards, marketing of credit cards to college students and many others, makes it clear that scholars find the theory useful and applicable to many practical decision-making environments.

JUSTIFICATION FOR ETHICAL OBLIGATIONS

ISCT stipulates that legitimate norms that are developed within communities are ethically binding on the members of the community. Although there are always the rights of exit and voice, some critics regard this as insufficient. Donaldson and Dunfee (1999: 42) also make provision for civil disobedience:

> Reasonably believing that an authentic norm of an organisation violates a hypernorm, a morally disgruntled employee could deny the legitimacy of the norm through a refusal to follow it. If indeed the norm violates a hypernorm, conforming to it is not ethically obligatory, and the dissenting employee is within her rights in refusing to follow the norm.

LACK OF A FULL-FLEDGED MORAL THEORY

John Boatright (2000: 456) is one of the critics who requires theoretical backup for ISCT and specifically for hypernorms. He argues that some ethical theory is required in order to know what hypernorms entail. Donaldson and Dunfee's (2000: 481) pragmatic response to this request is that it is "well-intentioned, but idealistic". They also do not seem too concerned about the absence of such a theory: "[W]hile the theory would be crisper and its results surely more transparent were such a background theory found, ISCT nonetheless adds considerable value without such a specification" (Donaldson & Dunfee, 2000: 482).

One of the benefits of a social contracts approach is that it makes provision for values that change over time and for existing contracts to be renegotiated. Donaldson and Dunfee (2000b: 437) explain how – in less than 50 years – the focus shifted from merely producing goods and services to expanded responsibilities such as fairness, quality of life, gender issues and work-life balance. Given the events that have taken place in the first decade of the twenty-first century, it seems likely that we are about to experience even more rapid change. It was mentioned above that Dunfee (2006: 310) acknowledges the contrary views on whether hypernorms can change over time.

A pragmatist's response might help. The following quote from Richard Rorty's address at the annual meeting of the Society for Business Ethics in 2005 provides an interesting perspective (Rorty, 2006: 371):

> God has provided no algorithms for resolving tough moral dilemmas, and neither have the great secular philosophers. Urging that there is something that makes actions wrong or moral beliefs true is an empty gesture. For we have no way of getting in touch with this purported truth-maker save to seek coherence among our own moral intuitions. Though truth and wrongness are not relative notions, justification is. For what counts as justification, either of actions or of beliefs, is always relative to the antecedent beliefs of those whom one is seeking to convince. Anti-slavery arguments that we find completely persuasive would probably not have convinced Jefferson or Aristotle. Our best arguments against torture would probably not have budged the devout and learned prelates who ran the Holy Inquisition. That is why we are sometimes tempted to say, misleadingly, that a certain practice is right in one culture and wrong in another, or that a certain astrophysical theory was true for Aristotle but false for Newton. The reason this turn of phrase is misleading is that all we really mean is that, given his other beliefs, Aristotle was perfectly justified in accepting a false theory. Analogously, the Mongol horde was perfectly justified in gangraping the women of Baghdad, given their other beliefs. Their behavior was, to be sure, wrong. If there were such a thing as absolute justification, we could say that it was absolutely unjustified. But there is no such thing.

To put our own contemporary values into perspective, here is an example of wisdom and experience from Victorian England. The following is an extract from a "Notice to Shop Assistants",[17] dating back to London of 1854:

- Any employee who is in the habit of smoking Spanish cigars, getting shaved at a barber's shop, going to dances and other such places of amusement will surely give his employer reason to be suspicious of his integrity and all round honesty.
- Each employee must pay not less than one guinea per year to the Church, and attend Sunday school every Sunday.
- Men are given one evening a week for courting purposes, and two if they go to prayer meetings regularly.
- After 14 hours work, spare time should be devoted to reading good literature.

17 http://funambulism.com/2008/02/notice-to-shop-assistants/, accessed 19 August 2013.

With the exception of smoking – for different reasons and not restricted to Spanish cigars – all these issues are unlikely to feature in contemporary ethical discussions or ethical codes. But they did form part of a legitimate micro contract more than 150 years ago.

A theory of business

In 2015, Tom Donaldson and Jim Walsh published an article titled "Toward a Theory of Business". The article attracted substantial interest in the academic world. I was at an Academy of Management Meeting in Boston, and a few sessions where they discussed this work were oversubscribed with people forming queues to gain access to the venues – not a common sight in academia!

The article revolved around an exploration of the purpose of business. Using the riddle "law is to justice, as medicine is to health, as business is to _____?", they offered the concept of Optimized Collective Value as their solution. This solution was based on what they described as a fallacy of composition – what is regarded as value for a single firm is not the same as value for business in general. They propose their theory of business (as a direct alternative to the theory of the firm) based on ideas about purpose, accountability, control and the nature of business success.

Donaldson and Walsh (2015: 197) provide the following comparison:

Although it was not their intention to take on the concept of creating shared value (CSV) introduced by Porter and Kramer, which was discussed earlier, it is very interesting to compare the two approaches. Figure 3.5 is my attempt to describe this in terms of the different ways in which we think about value (ethical values or economic value) and Donaldson and Walsh's distinction between value for a single firm and value for business in general. We can clearly see how CSV resonates with the creation of economic value, mostly of interest to single firms, whereas Optimized Collective Value addresses business in general and has a normative component.

Finally, it is important to look at a more recent contribution by Donaldson (2021), where he explores this normative component in more detail. He argues that the holy grail of integrating norms into management and organisation

Table 3.3 Comparison between the theory of business and neoclassical theories of the firm

Category	Theory of business	Neoclassical theories of the firm
Purpose	Optimise collective value	Maximise firm value
Accountability	To all business participants	To the law and to the firm's owners
Control	Prohibit assaults on participants' dignity	Guard against self-seeking with guile
Success	Optimized Collective Value	Shareholder wealth creation

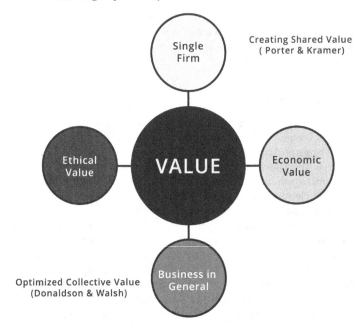

Figure 3.5 Views on value

remains elusive. He suggests that a practical inference framework can be useful by "seeking reasons rather than causes, and justifications rather than descriptions" (Donaldson, 2021: 1). This is discussed within the context of ongoing frustration about the complexities of the term "value creation", with specific reference to the dual interpretation referred to above. It is also emphasised, once again, that the process of *understanding* is an ongoing challenge.

Understanding is an internal, cognitive process. It does not entail any action and therefore – on its own – will not lead to any action. This illustrates the fundamental tension between theory and practice. In the famous words of Karl Marx: "The philosophers have only *interpreted* the world, in various ways. The point, however, is to *change* it."[18]

The statement by Marx is not supported by Marxists only. The sentiment is also shared by many corporations and their executives. That is the reason why the other dimensions in the proposed framework are described by *action* verbs: taking, governing, managing, reporting and regulating. With the

---

18 www.goodreads.com/quotes/17310-the-philosophers-have-only-interpreted-the-world-in-various-ways, accessed 21 November 2014.

exception of regulating (which is done by persons external to the corporation), the other verbs refer to actions that should be taken by the corporation itself. These are the actions that can be subjected to moral evaluation and are therefore the reason why corporations can be described as moral entities (Kaptein & Wempe, 2002: 125). With reference to the field of business ethics, Enderle (2007: 92) states the following: "[B]usiness ethics as part of humanities studies should excel in *action* orientation, focusing on philosophical reflection on the acting human beings and accounting for *all* important and interconnected determinants of our volition, thought and action."

References

Boatright, J. 2000. Contract theory and business ethics: A review of "ties that bind". *Business and Society Review*, 105(4), 452–466.

Bunnin, N. & Yu, J. 2004. *The Blackwell dictionary of western philosophy*. Malden, MA: Blackwell Publishing.

Button, M.E. 2008. *Contract, culture and citizenship: Transformative liberalism from Hobbes to Rawls*. Philadelphia: Pennsylvania State University.

Carroll, A. 1999. Corporate social responsibility: Evolution of a definitional construct. *Business in Society*, 38(3), 268–295.

Carroll, A. & Buchholtz, A. 2006. *Business & society: Ethics and stakeholder management*. Mason: Thomson South-Western.

Carroll, A., Lipartito, K., Post, J., Wherhane, P. & Goodpaster, K. 2012. *Corporate responsibility: The American experience*. Cambridge: Cambridge University Press.

Craig, E. (ed.). 1998. *Routledge Encyclopedia of Philosophy*. London: Routledge.

Crane, A., Palazzo, G., Spence, L.J. & Matten, D. 2014. Contesting the value of "creating shared value". *California Management Review*, 56(2), 130–153.

Donaldson, T. 1989. *The ethics of international business*. New York: Oxford University Press.

Donaldson, T. 2001. Values in tension: Ethics away from home. In Hoffman, M., Frederick, R. & Schwartz, M. (eds.), *Business ethics: Readings and cases in corporate morality*. Fourth edition. New York: McGraw-Hill, 475–483.

Donaldson, T. 2012. The epistemic fault line in corporate governance. *Academy of Management Review*, 37(2), 256–271.

Donaldson, T. 2021. How values ground value creation: The practical inference framework. *Organization Theory*, 2, 1–27.

Donaldson, T. & Dunfee, T. 1994. Toward a unified conception of business ethics: Integrative social contracts theory. *Academy of Management Review*, 19(2), 252–284.

Donaldson, T. & Dunfee, T. 1999. *Ties That Bind: A social contracts approach to business ethics*. Boston: Harvard University Press.

Donaldson, T. & Dunfee, T. 2000a. Précis for: Ties that bind. *Business and Society Review*, 105(4), 436–443.

Donaldson, T. & Dunfee, T. 2000b. Securing the ties that bind: A response to commentators. *Business and Society Review*, 105(4), 480–492.

Donaldson, T. & Walsh, J. 2015. Toward a theory of business. *Research in Organizational Behavior*. 35(181–207). doi:10.1016/j.riob.2015.10.002.

Dunfee, T. 2006. A critical perspective of intregrative social contracts theory: Recurring criticisms and next generation research topics. *Journal of Business Ethics*, 68, 303–328.

The Economist. 2005. The good company: A survey of corporate social responsibility, 22 January.

The Economist. 2008. Just good business: A special report on corporate social responsibility, 19 January.

Enderle, G. 2006. Corporate responsibility in the CSR debate. In Wieland, J. (ed.), *Unternehmensethik im Spannungsfeld der Kulturen und Religionen*. Stuttgart: Kohlhammer, 108–124.

Enderle, G. 2010. Clarifying the terms of business ethics and CSR. *Business Ethics Quarterly*, 20(4), 730–732.

Enderle, G. 2007. The ethics of conviction versus the ethics of responsibility: A false antithesis for business ethics. *Journal of Human Values*, 13(2), 83–94.

Enderle, G. 2014. Some ethical explications of the UN Framework for Business and Human Rights. In Williams, O.F. (ed.), *Sustainable development*. Notre Dame: University of Notre Dame Press, 163–183.

Freeman, E. 2002. Stakeholder theory of the modern corporation. In Donaldson, T., Cording, M. & Werhane, P. (eds.), *Ethical issues in business: A philosophical approach*. Hoboken, NJ: Prentice Hall, 38–49.

Freeman, E., Harrison, J., Wicks, A., Parmar, B. & De Colle, S. 2010. *Stakeholder theory – The state of the art*. Cambridge: Cambridge University Press.

Freeman, E., Martin, K.E. & Parmar, B.L. 2020. *The power of and: Responsible business without trade-offs*. New York, NY: Columbia University Press.

Friedman, M. 2002. The social responsibility of business is to increase its profits. In Donaldson, T., Cording, M. & Werhane, P. (eds.), *Ethical issues in business: A philosophical approach*. Seventh edition. Hoboken, NJ: Prentice Hall, 33–38.

Goodpaster, K. & Matthews, J. 1982. Can a corporation have a conscience? *Harvard Business Review*, January/February, 60(1), 132–141.

Hsieh, N.-H. 2004. The obligations of transnational corporations: Rawlsian justice and the duty of assistance. *Business Ethics Quarterly*, 14(4), 643–661.

Hsieh, N.-H. 2009a. Corporate social responsibility and the priority of shareholders. *Journal of Business Ethics*, 88, 553–560.

Hsieh, N.-H. 2009b. The normative study of business organizations: A Rawlsian approach. In Smith, J. (ed.), *Normative theory and business ethics*. Lanham: Rowman & Littlefield Publishers Inc., 93–118.

Kaptein, M. & Wempe, J. 2002. *The balanced company: A theory of corporate integrity*. Oxford: Oxford University Press.

Kell, G. 2013. *Executive director, UN global compact*. New York: Personal interview, 5 August.

Newton, L. (ed.). 2004. *Ethics in America: Source reader*. Second edition. Upper Saddle River, NJ (New York, NY): Pearson Education, Inc.

Parfit, D. 2011. *On what matters: Volume 1*. Oxford: Oxford University Press.

Porter, M. & Kramer, M. 2011. Creating shared value. *Harvard Business Review*, Issue HBR Reprint R1101C, 1–17.

Porter, M. & Kramer, M. 2014. A response to Andrew Crane *et al*'s article by Michael E. Porter and Mark R. Kramwer. *California Business Review*, 56(2), 149–151.

Rasche, A. & Kell, G. 2010. *The United Nations global compact: Achievements, trends and challenges.* New York: Cambridge University Press.

Rawls, J. 1971. *A theory of justice.* Cambridge: Harvard University Press.

Rawls, J. 2001. Justice as fairness. In Hoffman, M., Frederick, R. & Schwartz, M. (eds.), *Business ethics: Readings and cases in corporate morality.* Fourth edition. New York: McGraw-Hill, 53–59.

Rorty, R. 2006. Is philosophy relevant to applied ethics? *Business Ethics Quarterly,* 16(3), 369–380.

Schwab, K. 2008. Global corporate citizenship: Working with governments and civil society. *Foreign Affairs,* January/February, 87(1), 107–118.

Visser, W., Matten, D., Pohl, M. & Tolhurst, N. 2007. *The A to Z of corporate social responsibility.* Chichester: John Wiley & Sons Ltd.

Waddock, S. 2013. The future is here for the new CSR: Corporate responsibility and sustainability. In Zollo, M. & Mele, R. (eds.), *The shared value debate: Academic visions on corporate sustainability.* Milan: Egea, 37–46.

Williams, O.F. 2008. Responsible corporate citizenship and the ideals of the United Nations Global Compact. In Williams, O. (ed.), *Peace through commerce: Responsible corporate citizenship and the ideals of the United Nations Global Compact.* Notre Dame: Notre Dame University Press, 431–552.

Williams, O.F. 2014. *Corporate social responsibility: The role of business in sustainable development.* New York: Routledge.

Zollo, M. & Mele, R. (eds.). 2013. *The shared value debate: Academic visions on corporate sustainability.* Milan: Egea.

4 Taking responsibility

The first practical step in terms of responsibility is to *take* responsibility. This is the step that starts the thousand-mile journey, to use the famous quote of the Chinese philosopher Laozi (circa 604–531 BC). In this short chapter, taking responsibility is proposed as the transition from understanding to action. It links to the huge field of ethical leadership but does not address it in any detail.

A corporation has to make a conscious commitment to being responsible, displaying the understanding and committing to action. This action would usually be taken by the chief executive officer of a corporation in the form of a public statement. The commitment is the transition from the conceptual to the operational and is still in danger of being stuck in the empty space of words. It is a moment in time, and it is not immediately evident what will follow this critical step. It is like hitting the on switch without knowing whether the power is connected. Consider the following statement,[1] signed off by Ken Lay from Enron less than a year before the collapse of the company:

> As officers and employees of Enron Corp., its subsidiaries, and its affiliated companies, we are responsible for conducting the business affairs of the companies in accordance with all applicable laws and in a moral and honest manner. . . . We want to be proud of Enron, and to know that it enjoys a reputation for fairness and honesty and that it is respected. Gaining such respect is one aim of our advertising and public relations activities, but no matter how effective they may be, Enron's reputation finally depends on its people, on you and me. Let's keep that reputation high.

It is clear that the danger of lip service is present when a company *takes* responsibility, because the proof of the pudding will be in the eating. For example, acts of signing up to the UN Global Compact or other voluntary

---

1 http://bobsutton.typepad.com/files/enron-ethics.pdf, accessed 21 November 2014.

DOI: 10.4324/9781003356981-4

Figure 4.1 Taking responsibility

initiatives have often been questioned when there was no clear evidence of corporate commitment. For example, in South Africa there has been clear evidence of large-scale corruption at the electricity utility (Eskom), one of the first companies globally to sign up to the Compact, yet there has not really been any pressure on them to step down, at least as an interim measure.

Taking responsibility is about ethical leadership, and this concept will be discussed briefly below. But before we do that, a useful way to investigate the reasons for corporate commitment is to look at the distinction between the ethics of conviction and the ethics of responsibility, as introduced by the philosopher Max Weber in a famous lecture, "Politics as a Vocation", which he delivered to radical students in Germany in 1918 (Weber, 1971). Although the lecture was delivered with politics[2] in mind, the application to the role of the CEO of a corporation is just as relevant.

---

2 For a discussion on the links between democracy and governance, see Malan (2011).

The following view on capitalism comes from Weber's introduction to his book *The Protestant Ethic and the Spirit of Capitalism*:

> The impulse to acquisition, pursuit of gain, of money, of the greatest possible amount of money, has in itself nothing to do with capitalism. This impulse exists and has existed among waiters, physicians, coachmen, artists, prostitutes, dishonest officials, soldiers, nobles, crusaders, gamblers, and beggars. One may say that it has been common to all sorts and conditions of men at all times and in all countries of the earth, wherever the objective possibility of it is or has been given. It should be taught in the kindergarten of cultural history that this naïve idea of capitalism must be given up once and for all. Unlimited greed for gain is not in the least identical with capitalism, and is still less its spirit. Capitalism may even be identical with the restraint, or at least a rational tempering, of this irrational impulse. But capitalism is identical with the pursuit of profit, and forever renewed profit, by means of continuous, rational, capitalistic enterprise. For it must be so: in a wholly capitalistic order of society, an individual capitalistic enterprise which did not take advantage of its opportunities for profitmaking would be doomed to extinction.

Weber describes two different world views. The ethics of conviction presents the world of good intentions, sometimes exemplified by people acting on the basis of religious beliefs. For example: A Christian does what is right and leaves the outcomes to God. But the ethics of responsibility looks beyond conviction and intention and takes the consequences of action (or inaction) into account. In the words of Weber: "You should resist evil with force, otherwise you are responsible for its getting out of hand."

To some extent this distinction reflects the distinction between the business case and the moral case. If the commitment is based on the ethics of responsibility, the consequences of behaviour must be taken into account. That includes the consequences of profit made or lost, but it also includes the consequences of human suffering or environmental degradation. A committed CEO who wants to take responsibility in this way must therefore be able to practice what he or she preaches.

On the other hand, the ethics of conviction does not necessarily lead to action. The road to hell is paved with good intentions. The secular translation of this phrase might be: "A CEO does what is right and leaves the outcomes to the market."

However, the different outcomes from the two approaches are not very clear, perhaps because the market outcomes are so unpredictable. If, from a normative perspective, a CEO does what is right (e.g. disinvest from a country where human rights are abused), the action could be viewed as both a statement of conviction ("we will do this regardless of what happens to the share price") and an act of responsibility ("we are resisting evil with forceful action").

Enderle (2007) examines the famous lecture and – through a detailed discussion of Weber's position as well as the application of business ethics to Weber's points – comes to the conclusion that it is a "false antithesis" to declare that ethical standards must be based on either convictions or responsibility. He formulates his view as follows:

> Business ethics should persistently search for ways to act responsibly and effectively in the historical situation, neither escaping from the current situation into the inwardness of the soul or the nowhere of a dreamt-of better world; nor letting the epochal trends pass by with fatalism.
>
> (Enderle, 2007: 91)

Enderle's distinction is useful in assisting with a decoupling of the business case/moral case debate from the required operational approach to ensure efficacy. It also helps executives to take consequences into account without becoming consequentialists.

Taking responsibility is a moral act. It is based on an understanding of the moral purpose of business. It involves conviction and a sense of responsibility and requires ethical leadership. While the consequences are taken into account, they do not determine the decision. Rather, they determine the strategy. This signals the transition to the world of operations, more specifically the activities of governance and management.

Ethical leadership

As was mentioned in the introduction to this chapter, the field of ethical leadership is relevant here but not discussed in detail.[3] The concept has been more prominent in management literature. Ethical leadership is defined by Brown and Treviño (2006: 595) as "the demonstration of normatively appropriate conduct through personal actions and interpersonal relationships, and the promotion of such conduct to followers through two-way communication, reinforcement, and decision-making". In more straightforward terms, ethical leaders are described as "honest, caring, and principled individuals who make fair and balanced decisions" (Brown & Treviño, 2006: 597). In addition, Brown and Treviño (2006) mention that ethical leaders should be proactive role models and should engage in frequent communication about ethics, set clear ethical standards and use reward and punishment to ensure that such standards are followed. They make the distinction between a philosophical, normative approach (how leaders ought to behave) and their own

---

3 For an interesting discussion about the concept, see Grebe and Woermann (2011: 3), who argue that "ethical leadership . . . is a function of the more complex interaction of individual integrity, the institutions of integrity and the integrity of institutions".

social scientific approach that describes ethical leadership. They also compare the concept of ethical leadership with transformational, spiritual and authentic leadership and list the following as some of the key differences. According to Brown and Treviño (2006: 598) ethical leaders emphasise ethical standards and moral management while authentic leaders emphasise authenticity and self-awareness, spiritual leaders emphasise visioning, hope/faith and work as vocation and transformational leaders emphasise vision, values and intellectual stimulation.

Lawton and Páez (2015) define different dimensions of ethical leadership and distinguish between three interlocking circles: virtues, purposes and practices. They discuss the virtues of integrity and authenticity as two of the most important ones that appear consistently in the literature. They emphasise the importance of practices: "both integrity and authenticity are about doing, not just being" (Lawton & Páez, 2015: 642).

There are many examples of ethical leadership. One must be careful not to praise individuals too much, because the commentator's curse often applies. That is also why many companies with good reputations for corporate responsibility are hesitant to have their cases written up, for fear that praise will invite disaster. And Freeman et al. (2020) have also pointed out that we should get away from the "saints of sinners" dichotomy. Nobody's perfect.

Having said that, one of the best recent examples of comprehensive and substantive ethical leadership was provided by Paul Polman, the former CEO of Unilever. Polman has become an icon of ethical leadership, and the Unilever case study is indeed one that has been written up and studied by business students around the world. In an interview[4] with *Harvard Business Review*, Polman – as if scripted – uses the term "take responsibility"! He talks about "net positive leaders" and argues that they display the following characteristics:

> The first one is really that they take responsibility of that total impact in the world. I call it the total handprint, all consequences intended or not. Where we see some companies going wrong nowadays is that they celebrate and herald the positive sides of their business model. But when it gets to undermining democracy or hate speech or child addiction, they don't want to take that responsibility.
>
> Net positive leaders operate for the long-term benefit of business and society. Actually, they run their models just like we did in Unilever for the stakeholders. In fact, they believe in it so strongly that they can actually prove that by optimizing the return for all of the stakeholders, which includes the planet and future generations, they ultimately also satisfy

the shareholders, but they're not driven by the shareholders as their sole objective.

And then the net positive leaders are societal leaders. They understand that they need to play an increasing role in driving the broader systems changes, either at an industry level or with other partners . . .

So these are leaders that are very purpose driven leaders. They cherish the partnerships. They think multi-generational. They operate with a high level of compassion or empathy, humanity, humility. And it's interesting that these are also the leaders that have done well during this Covid crisis.

The last point to perhaps mention is that these leaders understand the importance of doing it everywhere in all parts of their business models, in all brands, in all operations, and they need to be consistent. And increasingly, companies that are consistent build that trust that is needed to drive prosperity.

Ethical leaders take responsibility. Then the real work starts.

References

Brown, M. & Treviño, L. 2006. Ethical leadership: A review and future directions. *The Leadership Quarterly*, 17(2006), 595–616.

Enderle, G. 2007. The ethics of conviction versus the ethics of responsibility: A false antithesis for business ethics. *Journal of Human Values*, 13(2), 83–94.

Freeman, E., Martin, K.E. & Parmar, B.L. 2020. *The power of and: Responsible business without trade-offs*. New York, NY: Columbia University Press.

Grebe, E. & Woermann, M. 2011. *Institutions of integrity and the integrity of institutions: Integrity and ethics in the politics of developmental leadership*. Developmental Leadership Program. [Online] Available: www.dlprog.org/publications/institutions-of-integrity-and-the-integrity-of-institutions-integrity-and-ethics-in-the-politics-of-developmental-leadership.php Accessed: 14 June 2015.

Lawton, A. & Páez, I. 2015. Developing a framework for ethical leadership. *Journal of Business Ethics*, 130, 639–649. https://doi.org/10.1007/s10551-014-2244-2.

Weber, M. 1971 (originally published 1930). *The protestant ethics and the spirit of capitalism*. Unwin University Book.

5 Governing and managing responsibility

The operational part of corporate responsibility signals the transition to practical activities. Making the assumption that a corporation has both a sophisticated understanding of responsibility and an authentic commitment to responsibility, backed up by the necessary ethical leadership, the action that is required will largely depend on two distinct activities: governance and management.

It is important to understand the differences between these two activities. Governance is, first and foremost, the responsibility of the board of directors, while management remains the responsibility of managers, some of whom may also be directors within the corporation. Depending on whether there is a unitary or dual board structure, the role of director can take the form of either an executive director or a member of the managing board.

Similar to the broader discussion about responsibility, it is important to understand both the conceptual components as well as the more practical standards that apply in various jurisdictions. The focus of this chapter is on the fundamentals of governance and management – relevant formal standards are important but will be dealt with mostly in the final chapter on regulation.

Corporate governance: the role of the board

There are many different definitions of corporate governance. One of the most useful and succinct definitions has been provided by Sir Adrian Cadbury and later adopted by the Organisation for Economic Cooperation and Development (OECD): "Corporate governance is the system by which companies are directed and controlled."

Because this definition has become the classical definition of corporate governance, it is useful to look at the more comprehensive definition as it appeared in the Cadbury Report of 1992 (Financial Reporting Council Limited, 2014: 1):

> Corporate governance is the system by which companies are directed and controlled. Boards of directors are responsible for the governance of their

DOI: 10.4324/9781003356981-5

Figure 5.1 Governing and managing responsibility

companies. The shareholders' role in governance is to appoint the directors and the auditors and to satisfy themselves that an appropriate governance structure is in place. The responsibilities of the board include setting the company's strategic aims, providing the leadership to put them into effect, supervising the management of the business and reporting to shareholders on their stewardship. The board's actions are subject to laws, regulations and the shareholders in general meeting.

International corporate governance expert and author of the book *The Fish Rots from the Head*, Prof Bob Garratt provides an extensive discussion of the history of the term governance, tracing it back to its Greek root of *kubernetes*, and describes how it has found expression in modern English through the concepts of not only governance and government but also cybernetics (Garratt, 2007: 151):

"Governance" is derived from the Greek kubernetes – the steersman. It gives us the notion of setting direction, of directing, the key to effective governance provided only that other people are willing to follow the

Figure 5.2 Governing responsibility

proposed lead. However, the original Greek gives us another modern word –
"cybernetics". This notion of an integrated system for steerage in turbulent
times has dropped out of fashion in the last two decades. I argue that it is
as important to modern governance as steerage. The two are inextricably
linked by the need for a system of learning.

A big problem with formalized governance standards is that there is often an
overemphasis on the control aspects; in other words corporations go into compliance mode and simply look for boxes to tick to fulfil the letter, but not the
spirit, of a particular standard. Once the performance aspect of governance is
understood, compliance does not necessarily take a back seat but takes up its
rightful place as one – but not the only – element of a governance system. The
focus on performance enables a more strategic understanding of governance,
which then makes it far easier for the board to become supportive – or even
excited – about its governance function.

The Swiss governance expert Prof Martin Hilb describes the difference
between the shareholder-focused (Anglo-American) model of governance
and the relationship-based model (e.g. Germany and Japan) which emphasises

stakeholder interests (Hilb, 2012). Hilb proposes a third, "new corporate governance" that integrates the strengths of both models. According to Hilb, this approach must be based on the following principles: situational, strategic, integrated and "keep it controlled" (referring to relevant auditing and risk management procedures).

Any model of corporate governance that acknowledges the importance of ethical principles and responsibilities to stakeholders other than shareholders would support the idea of the three fundamental corporate governance values of honesty, transparency and accountability (Garratt, 2003).

The learning board

Garratt's learning board model is a further development of the work of Bob Tricker and provides a useful summary of the role of the board of directors as well as the different aspects of corporate governance. Garratt reverses the strategic thinking and policy formulation components contained in Tricker's model, where strategic thinking was linked to the external perspective and policy formulation to the internal perspective.

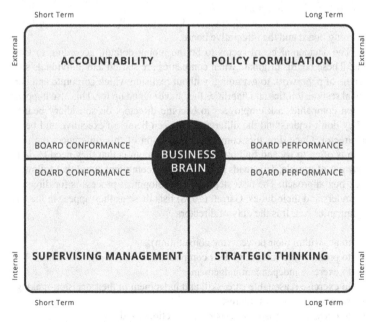

Figure 5.3 The learning board model

Source: Garratt (2003)

Using a basic matrix that maps short- and long-term perspectives against internal and external perspectives, Garratt describes how policy formulation (external focus and long term) and strategic thinking (internal focus and long term) combine to inform the performance aspects of corporate governance. In this context, policy formulation should be understood as the major policy decisions taken in terms of positioning the organisation in its external environment. This would include vision and mission statements.

Accountability (external focus and short term) and the supervision of management (internal focus and short term) jointly inform the conformance aspects of corporate governance. The role of the board as the "business brain" at the centre of the organisation is to ensure that these two aspects – performance and conformance – which have a natural tension between them, remain balanced. This tension is often described as the director's dilemma: deciding how to drive the enterprise forward while keeping it under prudent control (Garratt, 2007: 151).

Garratt (2007) explains the different levels of maturity that boards can achieve. He argues that there are four levels of maturity through which all boards need to develop before they can prove their competence and professionalism. According to him, an increasingly sceptical public view of board competence suggests that a conscious board development process is now a necessity and no longer simply an option.

He calls these the accidental board, the grumpily compliant board, the learning board and the integrative board.

The accidental board seems to be the global default, according to Garratt. These boards originate when companies are started and individuals sign reams of paperwork to get going, without realising which corporate and personal responsibilities and liabilities they have signed up for. This also happens when companies ask employees to become directors on subsidiary boards. They don't understand the difference between being an executive and being a director. Once directors come to a realisation of this difference, the next step is often to try and find out what the minimum is that they need to do to stay out of trouble. This leads to the grumpily compliant board that follows a tick-box approach. The next step in the development process is for directors to understand their duties. Garratt (2018) lists these as they appear in the UK Companies Act. It is the duty of directors

- to act within their powers (the constitution);
- to promote the success of their company;
- to exercise independent judgement;
- to exercise reasonable care, skill and judgement in their decision-making;
- to avoid conflicts of interest;
- to declare interests in third-party transactions; and
- not to accept benefits from third parties.

The next level is the learning board, which has already been described. This board understands the director's dilemma (driving the enterprise forward while keeping it under prudent control) and can focus on the four main tasks (Garratt, 2003):

• Policy formulation and foresight
• Strategic thinking
• Supervising management
• Ensuring accountability

Garratt (2018: 10) describes the final level of board maturity (the integrative board) as follows:

> The final level of board maturity, level three, is then to integrate the total organizational structure, processes, and climate to free the subsequent internal and external learning across all levels of the business. This is not just a nod to such fashionable notions as "creating a culture" – it is much harder-edged than that. The board commits to encouraging open learning across the organization that reflects the way the board itself is seen to be learning its role as the central processor of business information and the guardian of its strategy, values, and culture.

In a major theoretical contribution on governance, Donaldson (2012) discusses an "epistemic fault line" in corporate governance. He takes aim at the more traditional approaches of corporate governance – agency theory and transaction cost economics – and demonstrates how both commit the naturalistic fallacy of deriving an "ought" from an "is". Donaldson argues that the fault line separates positive concepts from normative concepts. He argues that these more traditional approaches to governance move from the "is" to the "ought" through a "ubiquitous sleight-of-hand that occurs when such theories transition from empirical *explanation or prediction* to prescriptive *guidance*" (Donaldson, 2012: 257). He uses a compliance-based definition of corporate governance, which is understandable mostly from a predominantly US perspective. Governance, according to him, is "the collection of rules, policies, and institutions affecting how a firm is controlled" (Donaldson, 2012: 257). His critique not only has important implications for the approach to governance but has wider applicability within the context of this book, with reference to the methodological stand-off that was discussed before (Donaldson, 2012: 265):

> [M]ore accurate empirical knowledge does not in itself add up to true advice. In itself, empirical knowledge contains no imperative or normative force. Epistemologically speaking, getting better advice about designing corporate

structures to minimize opportunism from knowing more about corporate behaviour and motivation is like getting better advice about how to lower one's golf score from knowing more about the physics of the golf swing.

Donaldson argues that the way to cross the epistemic fault line is to take seriously the distinction between explanation/prediction and justification. As soon as prescription comes into the picture (the "ought"), there is a need for normative justification (the "why"). According to him, the nature and structure of the world are not in themselves good or bad; they are good or bad solely in relation to human values. Normative preferences should therefore be made more explicit in theories of corporate governance (Donaldson, 2012: 266):

> [A]ny theory meant to guide corporations – that is, meant as a true theory of corporate governance – that fails to include some prescriptive support for corporate cooperation in the preservation of the natural environment, or that fails to involve, at least under certain circumstances, duties to refrain from damaging the integrity of the broader economic system, is inadequate.

This plea by Donaldson provides a perfect opportunity to introduce a few key international standards on governance.

Key standards and indices on governance

There are many international standards on corporate governance. The United Kingdom (UK) Corporate Governance Code and the Principles for Corporate Governance in the Commonwealth provide important perspectives. The European context is complex and dynamic. The significance of the South African King Reports on Corporate Governance extends to other parts of the world as well. The reason is that the King Reports, specifically the third and fourth King Reports (Institute of Directors in Southern Africa, 2016), have been acknowledged as international best practice, with specific reference to the area of corporate responsibility (or, in the language of the King Reports, corporate citizenship). Some global standards and/or guidelines with governance implications, such as the OECD, will be discussed in the chapter on regulation.

United Kingdom and Commonwealth standards

The Commonwealth is a voluntary association of 56 countries with a global span that includes Europe, Asia, Africa, the Caribbean and Americas and the Pacific. With a historic foothold in the British Empire and therefore not without controversy, the Commonwealth has a combined population of 2.5 billion people and, in 2021, had a combined GDP of US$ 13.1 trillion.[1]

---

1 For more information, see https://thecommonwealth.org/about/facts.

Within this context, it is useful to have a brief look at two relevant standards, the United Kingdom's Corporate Governance Code (formerly known as the Combined Code) and the Commonwealth Association for Corporate Governance Principles for Corporate Governance in the Commonwealth.

THE UNITED KINGDOM CORPORATE GOVERNANCE CODE

The UK Corporate Governance Code (formerly the Combined Code) sets out standards of good practice. In terms of Listing Rules, all companies with a Premium Listing of equity shares in the UK are required to report on how they have applied the Code. The standards relate to board leadership and effectiveness, remuneration, accountability and relations with shareholders.

The UK code also highlights the leadership and ethical responsibilities of the board (Financial Reporting Council Limited, 2014: 2):

> One of the key roles for the board includes establishing the culture, values and ethics of the company. It is important that the board sets the correct "tone from the top". The directors should lead by example and ensure that good standards of behaviour permeate throughout all levels of the organisation. This will help prevent misconduct, unethical practices and support the delivery of long-term success.

PRINCIPLES FOR CORPORATE GOVERNANCE IN THE COMMONWEALTH

The objectives of the Commonwealth Association for Corporate Governance are to promote good standards in corporate governance and business practice throughout the Commonwealth and to facilitate the development of appropriate institutions which will be able to advance, teach and disseminate such standards.

The 15 principles published by the Association are as follows:

> Principle 1 – exercise leadership, enterprise, integrity and judgment in directing the corporation so as to achieve continuing prosperity for the corporation and to act in the best interest of the business enterprise in a manner based on transparency, accountability and responsibility.

> Principle 2 – ensure that through a managed and effective process board appointments are made that provide a mix of proficient directors, each of whom is able to add value and to bring independent judgment to bear on the decision-making process.

> Principle 3 – determine the corporation's purpose and values, determine the strategy to achieve its purpose and to implement its values in order to ensure that it survives and thrives, and ensure that procedures and practices are in place that protect the corporation's assets and reputation.

Principle 4 – monitor and evaluate the implementation of strategies, policies, management performance criteria and business plans.

Principle 5 – ensure that the corporation complies with all relevant laws, regulations and codes of best business practice.

Principle 6 – ensure that the corporation communicates with shareholders and other stakeholders effectively.

Principle 7 – serve the legitimate interests of the shareholders of the corporation and account to them fully.

Principle 8 – identify the corporation's internal and external stakeholders and agree on a policy, or policies, and determine how the corporation should relate to them.

Principle 9 – ensure that no one person or block of persons has unfettered power and that there is an appropriate balance of power and authority on the board which is, inter alia, usually reflected by separating the roles of the chief executive officer and chairman, and by having a balance between executive and non-executive directors.

Principle 10 – regularly review processes and procedures to ensure the effectiveness of the corporation's internal systems of control, so that its decision-making capability and the accuracy of its reporting and financial results are maintained at a high level at all times.

Principle 11 – regularly assess the corporation's performance and effectiveness as a whole, and that of the individual directors, including the chief executive officer.

Principle 12 – appoint the chief executive officer and at least participate in the appointment of senior management, ensure the motivation and protection of intellectual capital intrinsic to the corporation, ensure that there is adequate training in the corporation for management and employees, and ensure that there is a succession plan for senior management.

Principle 13 – ensure that all technology and systems used in the corporation are adequate to properly run the business and for it to remain a meaningful competitor.

Principle 14 – identify key risk areas and key performance indicators of the business enterprise and monitor these factors.

Principle 15 – ensure annually that the corporation will continue as a going concern for its next fiscal year.

Again, the emphasis is on ethical leadership, transparency and a focus on external stakeholders, which are all hallmarks of the King Reports in South Africa. It is not surprising, then, to see that Mervyn King was the president of the Commonwealth Association for Corporate Governance at the time when these principles were published.

European standards

As mentioned above, the European context is complex, and with 28 member states of the European Union (EU) and 47 member countries of the Council of Europe, it is impossible to even scratch the service in terms of European standards. The European Commission Directive 2006/46/EC required listed companies in the European Union (EU) to include a corporate governance statement in the annual report to shareholders (International Finance Corporation, 2015). The EU Green Paper on Corporate Governance (2011) emphasised the importance of high-performing and effective boards and the need to challenge executive management where necessary. To be able to do this, boards need diverse skills, views and professional experience. The Green Paper also encouraged shareholders to take an interest in sustainable returns and long-term performance.

The International Finance Corporation (2015: 5) describes the corporate governance framework of the EU as a combination of legislation and soft law (codes). The European Corporate Governance Institute provides a comprehensive database of European corporate governance codes.[2] For a comprehensive overview and country-by-country analysis, readers are encouraged to look at *Corporate Governance in the European Union* by Chris Pierce (2010).

Institutional investors – the drivers behind ESG

There is an increasing focus on the role of investors in discussions about corporate governance in the context of responsible business. Especially institutional investors such as large pension funds and hedge funds play an important role. For example, Blackrock, one of the world's largest investment firms, has embraced ESG. The annual letter of its CEO, Larry Fink, to the CEOs of the companies in which they invest has become a popular icon of investor support for ESG. The following extract[3] from his 2022 letter is a good example of how

2 See www.ecgi.global/content/codes.
3 See www.blackrock.com/corporate/investor-relations/larry-fink-ceo-letter.

the ESG and broader stakeholder agendas have been integrated with hard-core investment decisions:

> Stakeholder capitalism is not about politics. It is not a social or ideological agenda. It is not "woke." It is capitalism, driven by mutually beneficial relationships between you and the employees, customers, suppliers, and communities your company relies on to prosper. This is the power of capitalism. In today's globally interconnected world, a company must create value for and be valued by its full range of stakeholders in order to deliver long-term value for its shareholders. It is through effective stakeholder capitalism that capital is efficiently allocated, companies achieve durable profitability, and value is created and sustained over the long-term. Make no mistake, the fair pursuit of profit is still what animates markets; and long-term profitability is the measure by which markets will ultimately determine your company's success.

This is an important development, because all too often managers or directors would use investors as an excuse to avoid responsible business practices. They would argue that they wanted to support such practices, but because they are under immense pressure from the owners of the corporation, they are not able to do anything about it. Responsible investment practices are therefore of huge importance, because these practices can have a major impact on the ability of corporations which want to conduct responsible business to do so, or to force corporations who do not want to, to do so as well.

Two investor initiatives that are of particular importance in this regard are the International Corporate Governance Network and the United Nations Principles for Responsible Investment.

INTERNATIONAL CORPORATE GOVERNANCE NETWORK

The International Corporate Governance Network (ICGN) is an investor-led organisation with the following mission: "[T]o inspire and promote effective standards of corporate governance to advance efficient markets and economies world-wide."[4]

This mission is pursued through three main activities:[5]

> Influencing policy by providing a reliable source of practical knowledge and experiences on corporate governance issues, thereby contributing to a sound regulatory framework and a mutual understanding of interests between market participants; [c]onnecting peers and facilitating cross-border communication among a broad constituency of market participants

---

4 www.icgn.org/about-icgn, accessed 22 November 2014.
5 www.icgn.org/about-icgn, accessed 22 November 2014.

at international conferences and events, virtual networking and through other media; and [i]nforming dialogue among corporate governance professionals through the publication of policies and principles, exchange of knowledge and advancement of education worldwide.

In 2021 the ICGN released an updated version of its corporate governance principles (International Corporate Governance Network, 2021). The document makes a distinction between the principles that apply to boards and those that apply to institutional investors, the so-called Global Stewardship Principles. The following are the ICGN Global Governance Principles (my own summary of each principle appears in parentheses):

Principle 1: Board role and responsibilities (the board should promote the long-term interests of the company for the benefit of shareholders with regard to relevant stakeholders).

Principle 2: Leadership and independence (board leadership requires clarity and balance in terms of board and executive roles).

Principle 3: Composition and appointment (the board should comprise a sufficient mix of knowledge, characteristics and skills to generate effective challenge and ensure objective decision-making).

Principle 4: Corporate culture (the board should demonstrate high standards of business ethics and integrity).

Principle 5: Remuneration (remuneration should align the interests of all employees with the company's strategy and purpose).

Principle 6: Risk oversight (the board should oversee risk assessment and disclosure).

Principle 7: Corporate reporting (the board should oversee disclosure related to the financial position, approach to sustainability, performance, business model, strategy and long-term prospects).

Principle 8: Internal and external audit (the board should establish rigorous, independent and effective internal and external audit procedures).

Principle 9: Shareholder rights (the rights of all shareholders should be equal and must be protected, with specific reference to minority shareholders).

Principle 10: Shareholder meetings (boards should ensure that meetings with shareholders are facilitated efficiently, democratically and securely).

It is clear that the ICGN expects its members to advance responsible investment practices, with specific reference to integrating ESG factors into investment decision-making. If members do this successfully it will create the space
for boards and managers to pursue these activities with the support of investors and therefore with much more effectiveness.

UNITED NATIONS PRINCIPLES FOR RESPONSIBLE INVESTMENT

The United Nations Principles for Responsible Investment (UN PRI) initiative has its historical roots in the UN Global Compact. The mission statement
of the UN PRI is as follows:[6]

> We believe that an economically efficient, sustainable global financial sys-
> tem is a necessity for long-term value creation. Such a system will reward
> long-term, responsible investment and benefit the environment and society
> as a whole. The PRI will work to achieve this sustainable global financial
> system by encouraging adoption of the Principles and collaboration on
> their implementation; fostering good governance, integrity and account-
> ability; and addressing obstacles to a sustainable financial system that lie
> within market practices, structures and regulation.

The six principles are:[7]

> Principle 1: We will incorporate ESG issues into investment analysis and
> decision-making processes;
>
> Principle 2: We will be active owners and incorporate ESG issues into our
> ownership policies and practices;
>
> Principle 3: We will seek appropriate disclosure on ESG issues by the enti-
> ties in which we invest;
>
> Principle 4: We will promote acceptance and implementation of the Prin-
> ciples within the investment industry;
>
> Principle 5: We will work together to enhance our effectiveness in imple-
> menting the Principles; and
>
> Principle 6: We will each report on our activities and progress towards
> implementing the Principles.

6   www.unpri.org/about-pri/about-pri/, accessed 22 November 2014.
7   www.unpri.org/about-pri/the-six-principles/, accessed 22 November 2014.

In 2021 the PRI had almost 4000 signatories with a total of US$120 trillion of assets under management.[8]

The King Reports

The King Reports on Corporate Governance contain non-legislated codes developed by the King Committee on Corporate Governance, a committee that was established by the Institute of Directors in Southern Africa. The King Reports have specific historical significance since the establishment of the King Committee coincided with the South African transition to democracy in 1994.

Named after the chairperson of the committee, Judge Mervyn King, the so-called King I (1994), King II (2004) King III (2009) and King IV (2016)[9] reports have received international recognition for being forward-thinking and innovative, especially in terms of recognising sustainability and corporate citizenship as key requirements for good corporate governance. There was also substantial progress from King I to King IV in terms of how the issue of ethics was handled. Whereas King I merely required a code of ethics (and actually provided a template!), King II emphasised the need to demonstrate a commitment to organisational integrity, while King III and King IV focused on the need for ethics practices to be integrated within the corporation.

Governance within an ESG framework

The rise of ESG is intertwined with new thinking about corporate responsibility and cannot be discussed in detail here. In short, the term was coined by the UN Global Compact in about 2004 and presented as a framework that would guide responsible investment. The term remained largely dormant for a very long time until about 2018, as illustrated by the Figure 5.4 below. In 2021 ESG surpassed CSR as a search term for the first time.[10]

Historically, ESG should be viewed in terms of the developing narrative about sustainability. In a sense, we have come full circle to understanding sustainability as a going concern, but in a world where ESG factors present real risks and opportunities. Figure 5.5 is my attempt to summarise this complex journey.

A sustainable company used to be one that could be described as a going concern but only with reference to financial performance. The introduction of the concept of sustainable development signalled a shift to environmental

---

8 www.unpri.org/download?ac=10948.
9 King III was released on 1 September 2009 and became effective on 1 March 2010. King IV was released on 1 November 2016 and became effective on 1 April 2017.
10 https://trends.google.com/trends/explore?date=all&q=ESG,CSR,Corporate%20Governance.

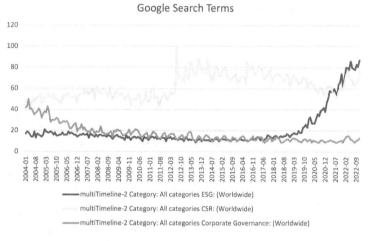

Figure 5.4 Google search terms history

Source: Google

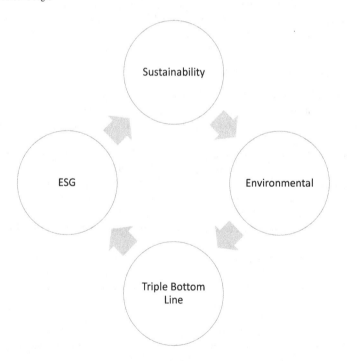

Figure 5.5 The conceptual journey of sustainability

issues, and this was further expanded through the triple bottom line and frameworks such as people, planet and profit, embraced by Shell in the 1990s. The arrival of ESG resulted in further changes in emphasis, but the adoption of ESG by the mainstream investment community also has significance from a normative perspective. Although not explicit, sustainable development and the triple bottom line have normative components. For example, the emphasis on future generations is certainly aligned with an ethics of care. The triple bottom line suggested broader measures of success and is aligned with stakeholder theory. Freeman denies that stakeholder theory is a normative theory and positions it as a pragmatic approach. The sleight of hand used by captains of industry was always to evade the issue by talking about enlightened self-interest. "Yes, we do this because it's good for business, but it is also the right thing to do." This only works up to a point because sometimes the two are not aligned. I referred earlier to this quote from the Brundtland report, which refers to tough choices.

> [S]ustainable development is not a fixed state of harmony, but rather a process of change in which the exploitation of resources, the direction of investments, the orientation of technological development, and institutional change are made consistent with future as well as present needs. We do not pretend that the process is easy or straightforward. Painful choices have to be made. Thus, in the final analysis, sustainable development must rest on political will.

Some of the ethical issues to be considered in the ESG conversation are the following:

- The current debate seems to be dominated by ideology, especially in the United States, and is often based on misunderstandings of what ESG investing is.
- A proper debate on ESG should acknowledge the existence of systemic ethical issues based on different world views.
- Honesty and transparency should inform the entire process, for example in terms of how products are defined and marketed. This includes the need for explainability and appropriate metrics, which will be discussed as part of the reporting dimension of responsibility.
- There is a need for fairness, specifically with reference to the avoidance of conflicts of interest.
- The G in ESG should be explored from a values perspective – although algorithms can calculate board diversity or levels of independence in seconds, sometimes discussions about accountability and stewardship are more important.
- Questions and discussions about corporate purpose should be encouraged. The ESG framework fits very well into the concept of Optimized Collective Value that was discussed in Chapter 3.

Managing: the role of management

The management of responsibility incorporates two main components: the management of corporate social responsibility, historically viewed as the external responsibilities of the firm towards society, and the traditional management of internal ethics (and compliance) programmes to ensure organisational integrity. Both of these are the responsibility of management, not the board. Very often these components are still divided along functional lines, where the corporate social responsibility function would reside within a public affairs or corporate communications department, and the ethics office would reside within the human resources or risk department. An approach that focuses on strategic CSR or shared value will not necessarily acknowledge these silos, but one has to recognise that there needs to be a functional division of labour to some extent.

The management of social responsibility as part of a public affairs department probably presents one of the biggest risks for a successful programme. Ironically, trusting the internal management of responsibility to those who are responsible to maintain and improve the reputation of the company can

Figure 5.6 Managing responsibility

have the exact opposite effect. The reason for this is that stakeholders are far more sophisticated and informed (and perhaps cynical) today than they were a decade or two ago. They can easily identify spinning exercises, and modern technology makes it possible for bad examples (good examples from the perspective of those looking for them) to go viral in a matter of hours. According to Waddock, social media forces business leaders to ensure that the public face of the company is authentic (Waddock, 2013: 40).

The management of corporate responsibility will be discussed first, followed by a discussion of the more traditional ethics management function and some suggestions on possibilities for convergence.

It is useful to revisit the steps thus far. Once a corporation understands the need for corporate responsibility, takes responsibility through a public commitment and ensures that the relevant governance mechanisms are in place, the main operational task is to manage responsibility. Given the increasing consensus that this is important for business as well as for moral reasons, the challenge for a corporation is to integrate these activities into its business practices. Apart from the operational challenges to get different business functions to collaborate, it is also to be expected that there will be a fair amount of resistance within the corporation. The understanding that might be present at the top does not always filter through to all levels inside the corporation.

Two of the most common characteristics of global best practice in corporate responsibility are that the programme was developed internally and that proper stakeholder engagement took place. Therefore, it is dangerous to study best practice with the intention to imitate, because – by implication – that would be bad practice. However, it is always useful to learn from companies which seem to get it right, as long as the organisation which is doing the learning realises that it has to learn (not copy) and adapt any practices that work elsewhere to fit local conditions.

With colleagues at the World Economic Forum, where I served as a member of the Global Future Council on Transparency and Anti-Corruption from 2019 to 2022, we conducted research on the global trend to move towards greater strategic intent and integration in terms of integrity management. In 2022 we published a White Paper (World Economic Forum, 2021) which was also translated into an academic paper (Malan et al., 2022), and suggested the following:

> While many companies view investment in governance simply as a means of staying out of trouble, proper corporate governance can – and should – drive company performance. To turn this idea into reality, a growing number of companies are moving toward a more holistic approach to ethical and responsible business. This involves aligning and coordinating across critical integrity functions, reducing box-ticking, and thinking holistically about ethical behavior, risk management and value creation.
>
> (Malan et al., 2022)

We based this statement on interviews with senior representatives of more than 20 global corporations. Our key findings of what leading companies are doing is that they have been working towards a more strategic approach to their ethical commitments. They do so via the appointment of leaders who oversee a broader set of functions, which include ethics and compliance, but are not limited to it. Rather, companies integrate functions and initiatives that relate to ethics and integrity, wherever they manifest in the organisation. Many of these activities have evolved from the more traditional position of an ethics and compliance officer. We know that companies have been expanding the role of compliance to include other ethical considerations for some time (Weber & Wasieleski, 2013). But there are noticeable regional differences. In the United States, for example, compliance is essentially an outcome of the 1991 Federal Sentencing Guidelines. As a result, early efforts to build ethical considerations were eclipsed by an overwhelmingly legalistic approach to these issues (U.S. Department of Justice Criminal Division, 2020). Compliance assumes that ethical challenges are principal-agent problems and that the primary risk to companies is a "bad apple" or rogue employee. As far back as 1994, Lynn Paine suggested that "rarely do the character flaws of a lone actor fully explain corporate misconduct". It has become increasingly obvious that this approach is not only culturally ineffective but also does not address a wider shift in public perception, whereby legal risk is no longer a good proxy for managing ethical issues. In other parts of the world, in contrast, a more comprehensive, integrity-based and stakeholder-driven approach has been present for a much longer time. This is especially the case in Western Europe and countries of the Commonwealth.

Regardless of the dominant historical framework, all companies in all regions are under greater pressure to respond to rising stakeholder concerns and frustrations, and there is not yet a clear consensus on the best way to do this. In particular, companies need to navigate situations where stakeholder views sharply diverge, presenting companies with strategic dilemmas, including what markets to operate in and which voluntary environmental and social commitments to observe.

The most visible manifestation of efforts to tackle these multifaceted challenges have led to the emergence of a senior leader who has responsibility for overseeing the *totality* of a company's integrity efforts and commitments – the Chief Integrity Officer (CIO).

The isolated act of simply appointing someone in the position of CIO will not be helpful. Rather, companies should take practical steps that are aimed at systemic and structural changes that would allow the CIO to flourish. The focus should be on consciously driving alignment between risk, compliance, governance, sustainability, investor relations, human relations, government affairs and corporate affairs. These are the four components we believe to be the most important.

Integration over silos

One of the most obvious and specific drivers behind the rise of a strategic approach to integrity is the new imperative to consider the totality of a company's regulatory and voluntary commitments and look for synergies between them. Today, meeting minimal legal commitments is far from sufficient for a company that wishes to be trusted and ethical. Companies are regularly pressed to take stands on controversial social and political issues, account for ethical violations deep in their supply chains and reduce the social and environmental harms of their business models. Further, issues that were previously managed according to "soft law" voluntary commitments are rapidly becoming a matter of "hard law". These include issues related to human rights, including trafficking, modern slavery, privacy and surveillance, supply chain oversight and disclosure of climate and other environmental risks. Finally, any operationalization of ESG or integrity commitments requires coordinated action across the business. All of these developments necessitate a more strategic approach to integrity and have driven the convergence of compliance and ESG oversight. Therefore, it does not make sense for integrity issues to be treated as a purely legal compliance issue. New ways of thinking about integration and integrity are crucial to improving communication, consistency, efficiency and effectiveness. They are vital to achieving sustainable success in the effort to create a culture of integrity.

Independence and autonomy

The CIO must be independent from commercial pressures and incentives. By now it is generally accepted that, while the compliance function is designed to represent the public interest, the legal department works in the interest of the company.[11] As we consider a more strategic approach to integrity, it must be equally clear that any commitments are not made solely based on calculations that they will drive growth and increased profit. While there is a "business case" for ESG and integrity more broadly, this does not mean that it will always be possible to quantify the commercial benefits (or ROI) of a particular initiative or decision. Any credible approach will consider trade-offs and make decisions with an understanding that (short-term) commercial benefit should not be the sole criterion.

Direct reporting lines to the board, a board committee, with oversight from the CEO, are ideal. Where the CIO reports to the chief legal officer, special attention should be paid to ensuring independence on the (relatively rare) occasions that the interests of the two functions diverge. Where one person

11 Griffith, S.J. (2016). Corporate governance in an era of compliance. *William & Mary Law Review*, 57, 2075–2140.

holds both the top legal and integrity roles, they must take great care to separate any diverging interests and consciously and pre-emptively assess priorities, preferably in consultation with senior leaders who can assure objectivity. This can be achieved through the creation of a committee (e.g. global integrity team, ESG steering committee) that meets regularly and functions as a sounding board or reality check. Some companies also create external advisory boards or stakeholder councils to ensure a critical external perspective on key decisions and formalise stakeholder consultation efforts. At no time can the CIO have profit and loss (P&L) responsibilities. Independence and autonomy from business pressures must be preserved, and appropriate leadership oversight and commitment must be guaranteed.

Seat at the table

The CIO must have a seat at the decision-making table for a number of reasons. The position requires insight into all major business discussions and decisions early on, to inform any risks related to goals, incentives and ambitions. As a member of the top leadership team, the CIO would have sufficient seniority and clout to hold the company's management accountable. Also, a seat at the table signals to employees that integrity is a priority to the leadership, which enhances the CIO's stature with employees, whether consciously or subconsciously. A direct line to the board of directors is ideal – not only to rectify any integrity issues at the C-suite level but, more importantly, to set a strategic direction for the organisation. Finally, the CIO can steer the board's attention to issues that are important to the company's overall strategy and lead the discussion on how to engage with stakeholders, and consider the trade-offs between their agendas and demands.

Critical skills and expertise

While the CIO will often have a legal background, that is not a requirement. What is essential, however, is that they be supported by a diverse and multidisciplinary team, with specific reference to skills related to technology, stakeholder engagement and the regulatory environment. Ideally, expertise of the team members should encompass law, behavioural science, organisational psychology, sustainability, human rights, data analytics, data visualisation, to name just a few. In addition, CIOs and their support teams should have high levels of emotional intelligence (EQ). To a large extent, this is a role that needs to be able to navigate organisational coordination and change, therefore EQ and soft skills are extremely important. Incumbents must be able to communicate complex issues to colleagues from different backgrounds, including people at all different levels of the company hierarchy, as well as third parties. They must be both proactive and reactive, and they must be naturally curious and open to new ideas and learning new skills.

Will ethics and compliance officers become extinct?

The rise of the CIO is a visible manifestation of a wider shift towards a more strategic and inclusive approach to integrity. It signals a fundamental shift in the responsibilities, rather than the replacement of ethics and compliance officers. It should therefore be viewed as an opportunity, rather than a threat, to existing ethics and compliance officers. Any effort to drive a more strategic approach to integrity will not begin in a vacuum but must build on the company's internal governance, structures and culture. But in order to be up to the challenge, those who are interested in this new and expanded role should ensure that they acquire the appropriate skills and expertise as rapidly as possible.

A practical framework for integration

Based on my own work with clients, in this final section I share some practical thoughts on how to integrate integrity into the core strategy, management and governance of companies. This approach uses a conceptual model that identifies four core areas that need to be addressed: assessment, behavioural change, compliance and disclosure. The final part (disclosure) obviously overlaps with the "reporting on responsibility" dimension.

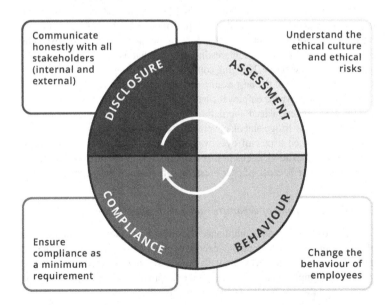

Figure 5.7 The ABCD framework

Assessment – understand your company culture and integrity risks

It is important to start with an assessment of the company's ethical culture and integrity risks. This will usually take the form of some form of a confidential survey that measures the following:

- Ethical misconduct: for example, excessive private use of company assets, unauthorized absence from work, violating internet or travel policies, etc.
- Specific behaviour that constitutes conflicts of interest, for example, accepting inappropriate gifts or hospitality, being related to a supplier, having a second job without proper authorisation or disclosure, etc.
- Behaviour prohibited by law, for example, accounting fraud, insider trading, procurement or tender fraud, etc.
- Perceptions about company culture, for example, familiarity with company values, effective ethical leadership, trust and accountability, company reputation, etc.

Behavioural change – getting people to do the right thing

Change is required to improve ethical *behaviour* and ethical decision-making skills. In this area it is useful to draw on the developing field of behavioural ethics, but the limitations of this approach should also be acknowledged. For example, one of the popular examples is to point out that most people will rate themselves as "above average" in terms of ethical behaviour, even though the logic of statistics determines that 50% of any population must always be below average. While this is interesting, it is not that useful from an integrity management perspective. Nudging could be explored as a way to improve ethical behaviour. One of the best examples is the experiment conducted at Newcastle University where employees had to pay for milk based on an honesty system. Researchers placed alternating photographs of either eyes or flowers on the door of the fridge and discovered that employees were up to four times more honest when a pair of eyes was staring at them! In this space there should also be acknowledgement that sometimes people with good intentions might misbehave because of peer pressure, ignorance or desperation.

Compliance – a point of departure rather than a destination

The need to move beyond compliance does not negate the critical importance of compliance itself. Companies need compliance as a basic foundation of integrity management. Technology plays an increasingly important role in this space, for example the use of blockchain to improve confidentiality in whistle blowing and the use of AI to support predictive disclosures.

Disclosure – without measurement and reporting you can't have trust

This is the final piece of the puzzle. Along all the other dimensions, data will be collected that will be used for reporting, either internally or externally. This includes the results of assessments, information on behaviour and compliance metrics. This data will feed into the bigger area of corporate reporting, which is addressed in the next chapter.

Ethics should not be seen as something peripheral to the organisation but should be part of normal business, should be reflected in all company policies and procedures and should be present in all decisions the company makes. The integration with decision-making is probably the most challenging. A formulaic interpretation of this requirement would necessitate decision-makers to pause before every decision and apply some form of an ethical screen, which is not a practical solution. Full integration, on the other hand, will be difficult to measure and could be abused. On this issue one often hears the following retort from a company executive: "Ethics is part of our DNA, we do not have to rely on policies and procedures." While perhaps describing an ideal state of affairs, it is too idealistic and borders on corporate spin.

Ethics management is a practical activity, and it is therefore useful to look at practical examples of ethical issues that need to be managed in organisations. Between 2005 and 2010, I collected more than 400 examples of ethical dilemmas from MBA students and participants in executive education programmes, mostly in a South African context. In addition, approximately 100 industry-specific dilemmas were collected from a large international professional services firm. These dilemmas were based on the real-life experiences of the individuals who agreed to share them, and were analysed with their permission.[12]

Here are a few of the dilemmas shared by the employees of the professional services firm:

- I have to deal with an employee who boasts about a promotion received after he threatened to resign.
- I do not comply with IT policies but am required to reprimand others who do the same.
- I have received complaints about a colleague who expects junior staff to work overtime while he goes home early.

---

12 Examples of dilemmas were collected after participants were exposed to a game of ethical dilemmas. The game, *Cards on the Table*, was developed by KPMG. Where permission was granted, the dilemmas have also been used in the development of an online ethics training programme (e-valuation) by Just Managing Consulting. More information is available at www. danielmalan.info.

- I have tried to work less overtime to spend more time with my family, but find that the quality of my work has suffered as a result.
- I do not get along with a colleague who really likes me.
- I have to decide whether to report two colleagues who have booked unauthorised flights.
- I have overheard two colleagues from the Information Technology Department discuss an easy way to cheat on a compulsory online test.
- A client has requested a reduction in fees, but I am not authorised to agree to such a reduction and cannot get hold of my superior. If I do not make a decision, we will lose the assignment.
- I have received documentation on a seemingly unimportant issue but do not understand the underlying assumptions and implications. I am hesitant to ask questions because this will make me look incompetent.
- I have discovered that a colleague has booked overtime for returning to the office in the evening to complete work after having taken time off during the day to attend to personal issues.

These dilemmas have been analysed according to a few basic matrices.[13] Although they do not constitute a representative sample, they do provide an interesting insight into the behaviour of employees. The analysis mapped that described behaviour against the following categories:

- Intent to do wrong: Is the description of the behaviour indicative of someone who had clear intentions to act unethically?
- Knowledge of policies: Is it evident (or likely) that the person who is acting (or considering an action) has sufficient knowledge of whether the particular behaviour would contravene a policy or not?
- Contravention of policies: regardless of whether the person had knowledge of the existing policy or not, was the relevant policy actually contravened?

Intent, knowledge and actual contravention

Figures 5.8 to 5.10 provide a basic analysis of all the dilemmas collected as part of this exercise.

---

13 Quite often people describe examples of ethical dilemmas as follows: "I have seen an example of misconduct in my organisation. What should I do about it?" In other words, the dilemmas are framed in such a way that the decision-maker has to decide whether to blow the whistle or not. Although it is impossible to prove, there is an assumption that often this type of description is provided to add a layer of protection to something that was experienced on a more personal basis, even though confidentiality is guaranteed during the collection of examples of dilemmas. This is similar to the idea of phoning a tax amnesty hotline and asking a hypothetical question or phoning on behalf of a friend. In interpreting each dilemmas, I have focused on the actual descriptions of the behaviour and not on the "do I report or not?" question.

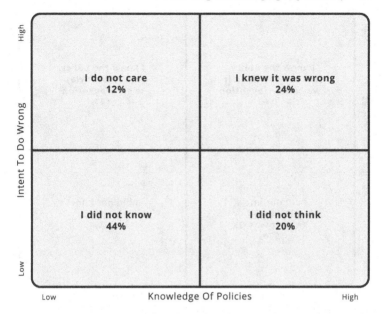

Figure 5.8 Analysis of dilemmas (intent and knowledge)

Figure 5.8 shows that, in 64 per cent of cases, there was a low intent to do wrong, and knowledge of policies presented a problem (66 per cent of these respondents did not have sufficient knowledge). However, in the case where there was clear intent to do wrong, 24 per cent of respondents actually had sufficient knowledge of the policies that they were going to contravene. This has clear implications for the design and implementation of corporate ethics training programmes, but that is not the purpose of the discussion here.

Figure 5.9 reveals that, in 44 per cent of the cases where respondents indicated that they had sufficient knowledge of the relevant policy, there was also an actual contravention of the policy.

Figure 5.10 indicates that in 24 per cent of cases where there was a contravention of policies, it did not coincide with an intent to do wrong. Also, in 12 per cent of cases there was intent to do wrong but no actual contravention of a policy.

To conclude this section, the following summary might be useful, although it is based on a generalisation. In any corporation, in the broadest possible terms, one can think of employees fitting into one of two categories in terms of their own approach to ethics: good (ethical) and bad (unethical). At the same time, employees' behaviour can be classified as good (ethical) and bad (unethical).

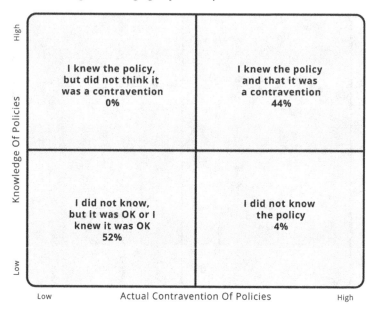

Figure 5.9 Analysis of dilemmas (knowledge and actual contravention)

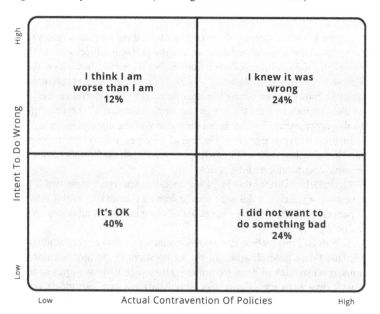

Figure 5.10 Analysis of dilemmas (intent and actual contravention)

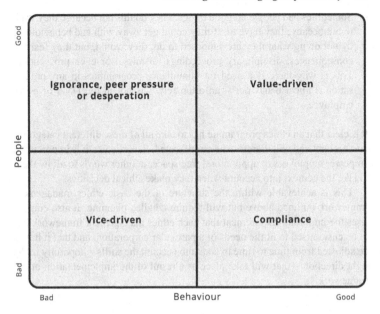

Figure 5.11 People and behaviour

Figure 5.11 presents a simplified matrix to illustrate the following four options:

- Good people do good things (values-driven). This is the ideal state in any corporation for obvious reasons, and any corporation would like to have as many employees as possible fitting into this category.
- Bad people do bad things (vice-driven). The employees who fit into this category are intent on harming the company through actions (either criminal or against company policy) that would benefit them at the expense of the company. It is unlikely that conventional ethics management programmes will have much effect on their behaviour. There are usually not too many employees that belong in this category.
- Sometimes good people do bad things. This could be the result of ignorance or pressure. The employees in this category need assistance in a very specific way: training on the contents of relevant policies, ethical decision-making skills to enable them to make the right decision and empowerment to be able to speak up[14] when colleagues or supervisors pressurise them to act unethically.

---

14 Although a whistle-blowing hotline is the more accustomed way of speaking up, and also offers the opportunity of doing so anonymously, there are other ways of speaking up directly by raising

- Sometimes bad people do good things. They do this not because they want to but because they have to. If they could get away with bad behaviour or by not doing what they are supposed to do, they would, but they fear the consequences: disciplinary proceedings, dismissal or even prosecution. This is why there is a need for compliance programmes in any organisation. Ethical behaviour – unfortunately – is not in the DNA of every employee.

It is clear that an ethics programme has to take all of these different categories into account and will therefore be multifaceted. In particular, it is important to empower employees to apply moral free space, in other words to allow them to take the context into account when they make ethical decisions.

This is achievable within the structure of the basic ethics management framework outlined above but will require detailed planning. It also emphasises the important requirement that each ethics management framework has to be customised to fit the needs of a particular corporation, and that it has to be adjusted from time to time to take into account the shifts – hopefully in the right direction – that will take place as a result of the implementation of the framework.

CODES

In terms of an ISCT framework, the development of company-specific codes should be highlighted. On condition that they are developed properly, with extensive stakeholder engagement being one of the critical requirements – they can be viewed as micro contracts. In the case of multinational corporations, there is a more complex structure involved, because there is often a global code supported by regional or country-specific codes. This provides an ideal opportunity for the application of ISCT, where the global code could be viewed as a macro contract (within a very specific context), supported by micro contracts. For corporations that are members of the UN Global Compact, the same structure can be applied, with the UN Global Compact being the macro contract and the company code a micro contract.

I was involved in the process of developing the KPMG Global Code of Conduct a number of years ago. A very specific example of how moral free space can be applied is provided in this case. The global code stated clearly that the firm is opposed to discrimination in all its forms, while, at the same time, the regional code for southern Africa (a separate document that was developed for affiliated firms in the region) included support for affirmative

---

difficult issues and inviting discussion. The work of Mary Gentile has been very influential in this area, specifically the development of her "Giving Voice to Values" curriculum. More information is available at www.givingvoicetovaluesthebook.com/.

action in South Africa and for localisation practices in Botswana. These are very specific issues that are relevant only at the regional level and therefore could be defined as moral free space.

In a 2004 study of the 200 largest corporations in the world, it was found that only 52.5 per cent of them had codes (Kaptein, 2004). But about 10 years later, Sharbatoghlie et al. (2013) found that 95 per cent of both Fortune US 100 and Fortune Global 100 companies had a code of ethics.

Three different types of codes are identified by Kaptein (2004: 13): the stakeholder statute, the values statement and the code of conduct (Kaptein, 2004: 13). Stakeholder statutes have both an internal and external focus and aim to clarify responsibilities and principles towards stakeholders. Values statements are primarily for internal use and to a lesser extent for external use and promote organisational values. Codes of conduct are primarily for internal use and describe desirable employee conduct (Kaptein, 2004: 25).

The stakeholder principles that were most often addressed in the codes are (percentage in parentheses indicates the percentage of companies that cited the principle in their code: transparency (55 per cent), honesty/truth (50 per cent), fairness/impartiality (45 per cent), trust (23 per cent) and empathy/respect/diversity (20 per cent) (Kaptein, 2004: 21).

Kaptein (2004: 26) argues that the wide diversity that was found in terms of structure and content is not a negative but can be interpreted as an indication of authenticity, that is, it indicates that corporations developed their own documents and took local conditions into account. Although this is not the same as an indication of the application of moral free space, at least the findings are compatible with the application of moral free space.

In a study performed by Paine et al. (2005), they describe the value of a code as follows: By adopting its own code, a company can clarify for all parties, internal and external, the standards that govern its conduct and can thereby convey its commitment to responsible practice wherever it operates.

Paine et al. (2005) developed a Global Business Standards Codex as a benchmark for companies that want to create a code. They define eight principles that define best practice (I have included practical examples of issues addressed by codes in brackets):

- Fiduciary principle (e.g. conflicts of interest)
- Property principle (e.g. theft of company assets)
- Reliability principle (e.g. keeping promises and being trustworthy)
- Transparency principle (e.g. being honest and truthful)
- Dignity principle (e.g. human rights)
- Fairness principle (e.g. fair competition, bribery and corruption)
- Citizenship principle (e.g. respect for the rule of law and responsible engagement on public and societal issues)
- Responsiveness principle (e.g. supply chain integrity or customer treatment)

A brief case study

An early example of an attempt to integrate the management of ethics and the management of corporate responsibility was provided by Barclays about a decade ago. As one of the biggest financial services companies in the world, Barclays was confronted by a series of scandals that prompted changes at the executive level and a complete rethink of its position on corporate responsibility.

The major scandal involved the manipulation of the LIBOR rate (the London inter-bank lending rate). In June 2012 Barclays was fined £290 million for attempts by some of its derivative traders to rig the rate. This resulted in the resignation of both Barclays Chief Executive Bob Diamond and Chairman Marcus Agius.

At first the chief executive, Bob Diamond, resisted pressure to resign. In a letter to staff a few days after the huge fine was imposed, he wrote:[15]

> I love Barclays, and I am proud of all of you. We all know that these events are not representative of our culture, and it is my responsibility to get to the bottom of that and resolve it. Make no mistake the actions taken in this incident were against all of the principles we live by.

One day later he resigned. Agius, who had earlier resigned as chairman, was asked to step in as caretaker chief executive. The incoming chief executive, Antony Jenkins, initiated a series of sweeping reforms inside the bank, with a specific focus on corporate citizenship.[16]

Jenkins[17] stated that "people rightly expect businesses to demonstrate leadership by serving as a catalyst for helping societies to prosper. Barclays is committed to meeting that responsibility". The Barclays Citizenship Plan (Barclays plc, 2013) outlines a citizenship strategy that is based on three key pillars. These are called "The way we do business", "Contributing to growth", and "Supporting our communities". This structure manages to address many of the challenges discussed in this section.

"The way we do business" addresses the link between corporate responsibility issues and internal ethics requirements. The Citizenship Plan defines "The way we do business" as follows:

- We will: implement a global Code of Conduct to set clear and consistent expectations of behaviour.
- We will: ensure material business decisions reflect stakeholder considerations

---

15 www.bbc.com/news/business-18678731, accessed 23 November 2014.
16 To ensure transparency, the writer discloses that he is a consultant to Barclays Africa. However, he was not involved in the design of the three pillar model on corporate citizenship.
17 www.resources.barclays.com/citizenshipreport/, accessed 23 November 2014.

- We will: proactively manage the environmental, social and governance impacts of our business
- We will: be market leading on transparency – being as open as possible about how we do business
- We will: minimise our broader systemic risk to the economy and society

"Contributing to growth" addresses the link between corporate responsibility and the broader economy. It emphasises (implicitly) the fact that responsible business behaviour and corporate citizenship are strategic issues and can be used to make a contribution to growth while making profit at the same time. The Citizenship Plan defines "Contributing to growth" as follows:

- We will: leverage our products, capital networks and expertise to drive sustainable progress
- We will: help more businesses to start-up and grow
- We will: improve youth employability

And finally, "Supporting our communities" refers to the more traditional CSR activities that many corporations offer. It is important to note that these activities are not discarded altogether, but rather, they are given a new context as one of three pillars. The Citizenship Plan defines "Supporting our communities" as follows:

- We will: invest £250 million in community programmes
- We will: help build the enterprise, employability and financial skills of five million disadvantaged young people

Taken together, this approach demonstrates integration at two distinct levels. Firstly, there is the integration of ethics management and corporate citizenship. "The way we do business" is positioned as a fundamental component of citizenship. Secondly, there is integration between citizenship activities and the contribution that the corporation can make to the economy. In other words, there is a strategic link between responsible business and successful business.

This approach can be regarded as best practice. It has received a lot of airtime within the bank through communication and training. But it is not a magic wand that will solve all the problems of Barclays. Two years after the LIBOR scandal, Barclays made headlines again, this time with regard to the so-called dark pools (a vehicle that allows investors to trade big blocks of shares anonymously). In June 2014, a lawsuit was filed in the United States by the New York State attorney general, which alleged that Barclays had promised to get the best possible prices for customers looking to buy or sell shares, but that it had instead taken steps that maximised the bank's profits. The bank's share value dropped by 5 per cent in one day, but Antony Jenkins was protected because the alleged misconduct took place before he took over as chief executive.

The Barclays case provides good insight into the complexity of corporate responsibility issues in the current environment. It is extremely challenging to manage the behaviour of a multinational corporation with approximately 140,000 employees, operating in many jurisdictions around the world. Cultural problems in a huge organisation are complex. Progress is likely to be incremental, and because of different agendas from different stakeholders, there will be fundamental differences on what exactly constitutes an improvement in culture and how it could be measured.

In 2016, Barclays reported that it had met or exceeded 10 of the 11 goals.[18] The statement of purpose of Barclays[19] has remained unchanged for about a decade:

> Finance is the oxygen of the economy. Acting transparently and with expertise, we *deploy finance responsibly to support people and businesses*. We have the capability and capital, the operational resilience and the commitment, to make a real and lasting difference to the economic lives of customers and communities. This is as true today as it was when our bank was founded over 330 years ago.
>
> *Acting with empathy and integrity*, we aim to be a leader in the profession of banking and to engender trust amongst our key stakeholders. We understand the power of building a supportive and inclusive culture for everybody, knowing that we make a bigger difference when we pull together as one team.
>
> We operate with energy and imagination, *championing innovation and sustainability*, to make a positive and enduring difference, to take pride in leaving things better than we found them. New ideas and technologies can help customers and communities to unlock opportunities.
>
> Our success is judged not only by commercial performance, but also by our contribution to society, and how we act responsibly *for the common good and the long term*, because these outcomes are mutually dependent. We are at our best when our clients, customers, communities, and colleagues all progress.

Of course, a purpose statement such as this one should be subjected to scrutiny. In the introduction I alluded to the fact that writing is always at least one step removed from performance. One of the best ways to illustrate this is to revisit the lofty words from Enron CEO Ken Lay that was quoted earlier.

---

18 See www.3blmedia.com/news/barclays-concludes-four-year-citizenship-plan.
19 See https://home.barclays/who-we-are/our-strategy/purpose-and-values/.

In retrospect, it is easy to spot the irony. But how do we know that any information provided by a corporation is accurate and reliable? That relies on measurement and reporting, which is the topic of the next chapter.

References

Donaldson, T. 2012. The epistemic fault line in corporate governance. *Academy of Management Review*, 37(2), 256–271.

European Union. 2011. *Green Paper: The EU corporate governance framework*. Brussels. [Online] Available https://op.europa.eu/en/publication-detail/-/publication/3eed7997-d40b-4984.

Financial Reporting Council Limited. 2014. *The UK Corporate Governance Code*. [Online] Available: www.frc.org.uk/Our-Work/Publications/Corporate-Governance/UK-Corporate-Governance-Code-2014.pdf Accessed: 14 June 2015.

Garratt, B. 2003. *The Fish Rots from the Head*. London: Profile Books.

Garratt, B. 2007. Directors and their homework: Developing strategic thought. *International Journal of Business Governance and Ethics*, 3(2), 150–162.

Garratt, B. 2018. *The four levels of board maturity*. [Online] Available: https://garrattlearningservices.files.wordpress.com/2018/09/four-levels-of-board-maturity-sept-2018.pdf.

Hilb, M. 2012. *New corporate governance*. Fourth edition. Berlin: Springer.

Institute of Directors in Southern Africa. 2016. *The king report on corporate governance in South Africa*. Johannesburg: Institute of Directors in Southern Africa. [Online] Available: www.iodsa.co.za/page/king-iv

International Corporate Governance Network. 2021. *ICGN global governance principles*. London: International Corporate Governance Network. [Online] Available: www.icgn.org/sites/default/files/2021-11/ICGN%20Global%20Governance%20Principles%202021.pdf.

International Finance Corporation. 2015. *A guide to corporate governance practices in the European Union*. Washington, DC: International Finance Corporation. [Online] Available www.ifc.org/wps/wcm/connect/506d49a2-3763-4fe4-a783-5d58e37b8906/CG_Practices_in_EU_Guide.pdf?MOD=AJPERES&CVID=kNmxTtG.

Kaptein, M. 2004. Business codes of multinational firms: What do they say? *Journal of Business Ethics*, 50, 13–31.

Malan, D., Taylor, A., Tunkel, A. & Kurtz, B. 2022. *Why business integrity can be a strategic response to ethical challenges*. MIT Sloan Management Review. [Online] Available:https://sloanreview.mit.edu/article/why-business-integrity-can-be-a-strategic-response-to-ethical-challenges/.

Paine, L. 1994. Managing for organizational integrity. *Harvard Business Review*, 72(2), 106–117.

Paine, L., Deshpandé, R., Margolis, D. & Bettcher, K. 2005. Up to code: Does your company's conduct meet world class standards? *Harvard Business Review*, December 2005.

Pierce, C. 2010. *Corporate governance in the European Union*. Orpington: Global Governance Services Ltd.

Sharbatoghlie, A., Mosleh, M. & Shokatian, T. 2013. Exploring trends in the codes of ethics of the fortune 100 and global 100 corporations. *Journal of Management Development*, 32(7), 675–689.

U.S. Department of Justice Criminal Division. 2020. *Evaluation of corporate compliance programs.* [Online] Available: www.justice.gov.

Waddock, S. 2013. The future is here for the new CSR: Corporate responsibility and sustainability. In Zollo, M. & Mele, R. (eds.), *The shared value debate: Academic visions on corporate sustainability.* Milan: Egea, 37–46.

Weber, J. & Wasieleski, D. 2013. Corporate ethics and compliance programs: A report, analysis and critique. *Journal of Business Ethics,* 112(2013), 609–626.

World Economic Forum. 2021. *The rise and role of the chief integrity officer.* [Online] Available:https://www3.weforum.org/docs/WEF_The_Rise_and_Role_of_the_Chief_Integrity_Officer_2021.pdf.

6 Reporting on responsibility

Corporate reporting is of particular importance because it provides the window on all the other dimensions of responsibility. A corporate report shares information – financial or non-financial – with both external and internal stakeholders. It is through the analysis of corporate reports that stakeholders and scholars receive insight into how corporations understand, take, govern and manage responsibility.

This chapter provides a brief historical overview of sustainability reporting and contextualises the emergence of the concept of integrated reporting. The business case for reporting and the main role players and standards are discussed, with specific reference to the rapid consolidation that has taken place over the last few years, resulting in the establishment of the International Sustainability Standards Board in 2021.

The evolution of reporting

Corporate responsibility reporting has been around for longer than many people might think. Over time, the focus has shifted from social components, to environmental components, to a "triple bottom line" approach. The triple bottom line (TBL or 3BL) was coined by John Elkington in the 1990s to describe the need for companies to measure performance in terms of social, environmental and economic impact.[1]

Over the last decade there has been a focus on the concept of integrated reporting, but currently the emphasis has swung back to sustainability reporting. The roots of reporting can be traced back to the 1940s when the term "social audit" was used for the first time by Stanford's Professor Theodore Kreps (1897–1981) in relation to companies reporting on their social responsibilities. This concept was further developed during the 1950s and beyond, but mostly within academic circles and focused on the broader concept of

---

1 Interestingly, in 2018 Elkington suggested a voluntary recall to finetune the concept. See https://hbr.org/2018/06/25-years-ago-i-coined-the-phrase-triple-bottom-line-heres-why-im-giving-up-on-it.

DOI: 10.4324/9781003356981-6

Figure 6.1 Reporting on responsibility

corporate social responsibility (CSR), as opposed to the activities of measurement and reporting.

During the 1980s, ethical investment funds in the United Kingdom and the United States of America (USA) started screening companies based on their social and ethical performance. The 1990s brought increased reporting; for example, the Body Shop International voluntarily published its first Values Report in 1995. The Body Shop report included environmental, animal protection and social statements. The 1990s were described as the "Transparency Decade" by the globally recognised think tank SustainAbility. This was a period when a series of major incidents forced pioneering companies to "come clean" and issue reports. At the same time, sustainability reporting standards were formalised through the Global Reporting Initiative (GRI). SustainAbility argued that the first decade of the twenty-first century might become the "Trust Decade", based on ever-increasing transparency, accountability and reporting. Ironically, this decade turned out to be one of fundamental distrust, starting with the collapse of Enron and ending with the aftermath of the global financial crisis. It could perhaps be argued that the distrust arose as a result of increased disclosure and transparency. However, a more plausible reason is that poor or questionable corporate performance (rather than increased disclosure) was the main culprit. The most recent decade was characterized by the establishment of multiple role players, including the establishment of the Sustainability Accounting Standards Board (SASB) and the International Integrated Reporting Committee (IIRC). All of these, with the exception of the GRI, have now been folded into the International Sustainability Standards Board and will be discussed below.

The most important changes that have been identified over the last few decades are the growth in the number of reporting companies (from a few dozen to a few thousand), the shift from environmental disclosure to triple-bottom-line disclosure to integrated reporting and the rapid increase in the volume of information (initially mostly printed but currently almost exclusively online).

KPMG International (2022) estimates that almost all of the 250 largest companies in the world are now issuing annual sustainability reports. In their biannual research they also measure trends of the top 100 companies by revenue in 58 different countries, the so-called N100 companies. The percentage of N100 companies issuing sustainability reports has grown from 64 per cent to 79 per cent over the last decade.

KPMG (2022) identifies the following global trends:

- A move towards standards framed by stakeholder materiality assessments.
- Increased reporting on climate-related risks and carbon reduction targets.
- Growing awareness of biodiversity risks.
- A preference for quantity over quality in terms of the reporting on the UN SDGs.
- A secondary role for social and governance risks compared to climate risks.

Smith and Alexander (2013) analysed website headings of Fortune 500 companies to determine which CSR-related headings are the most common. They found the words "community" and "environment" to dominate the headings, with 83 per cent and 80 per cent of Fortune 500 companies respectively using these terms as headings on their websites. There was a substantial drop to the next level of headings used: health and wellness (63 per cent), sustainability (62 per cent), diversity (60 per cent) and ethics (59 per cent). The headings of corporate responsibility (36 per cent) and citizenship (17 per cent) were used relatively infrequently (Smith & Alexander, 2013: 163).

The challenge that was identified by SustainAbility some time ago remains relevant today, namely the need to link sustainability issues with business performance and corporate identity. More recently the positions of financial institutions and institutional investors have made a substantial contribution to highlighting the business case for reporting, with the UN Principles for Responsible Investment (an initiative of the UN Global Compact and UNEP

Finance Initiative) and the International Corporate Governance Network (ICGN) being particularly active in this regard.

Over the years there have been increasing requests for governments to make some form of sustainability reporting compulsory. Extensive lobbying succeeded in putting reporting on the agenda for the Rio+20 Earth Summit in 2012. In the end, a relatively watered-down paragraph was inserted in the final declaration[2] signed by 114 heads of state. Paragraph 47 of the final declaration reads:

> We acknowledge the importance of corporate sustainability reporting and encourage companies, where appropriate, especially publicly listed and large companies, to consider integrating sustainability information into their reporting cycle. We encourage industry, interested governments as well as relevant stakeholders with the support of the UN system, as appropriate, to develop models for best practice and facilitate action for the integration of sustainability reporting, taking into account the experiences of already existing frameworks, and paying particular attention to the needs of developing countries, including for capacity building.

Following agreement with this wording, France, Denmark, South Africa and Brazil cooperated in forming a governmental group entitled the "Group of Friends of Paragraph 47". The group published a Charter[3] in which they emphasised the value of regulation, the topic of the final chapter of this book:

> Based on several national experiences, we are of the view that the development of models of best practice on policy and market regulation on corporate sustainability reporting is an important step towards making sustainability reporting widespread practice. Policy and regulation will level the playing field and create enabling conditions for the business sector to contribute to sustainable development.

In addition, the OECD Guidelines for Multinational Enterprises recommend the following (OECD, 2011: 27):

> Enterprises should ensure that timely and accurate information is disclosed on all material matters regarding their activities, structure, financial situation, performance, ownership and governance. This information should be disclosed for the enterprise as a whole, and, where appropriate, along

2 www.un.org/disabilities/documents/rio20_outcome_document_complete.pdf, accessed 8 June 2014.
3 www.unep.org/resourceefficiency/Portals/24147/Business-Ressource%20Efficency/GoF47%20 Two-Pager.pdf, accessed 8 June 2014. Also see https://wedocs.unep.org/bitstream/handle/20.500.11822/26175/GoF47_Charter.pdf?sequence=1&isAllowed=y.

business lines or geographic areas. Disclosure policies of enterprises should be tailored to the nature, size and location of the enterprise, with due regard taken of costs, business confidentiality and other competitive concerns.

In a speech to the Institute of Chartered Accountants in England and Wales in March 2014, Mervyn King, former chairman of the IIRC, explained the responsibility of the board to ensure that traditional reporting is translated into a more accessible format:[4]

> To be accountable, the board must report in an understandable manner. Financial and non-financial reporting are each critical but neither alone nor in their silos is sufficient. The system of [integrated reporting] requires the board to apply its collective mind to those reports prepared, to the average user, in incomprehensible language, understand them and explain "the state of play" of the company in clear, concise and understandable language. Such a report enables all stakeholders to make an informed assessment about the company's stability and sustainability.

A 2020 publication of the United Nations Environment Programme (UNEP), the Centre for Corporate Governance in Africa at the University of Stellenbosch Business School, the GRI and KPMG, namely *Carrots and sticks – Sustainability Reporting Policy: Global trends in disclosure as the ESG agenda goes mainstream*, indicated an increase in mandatory reporting standards in many developed and developing countries. The report identified 614 reporting provisions globally, of which almost 40 per cent came from Europe.[5]

Seventy-two per cent of the 180 reporting-related standards or policies that were identified in the 45 reviewed countries were mandatory (UNEP et al., 2013).

The European context is the one where mandatory reporting practices are most advanced. The Corporate Sustainability Reporting Directive (2022/2464/EU) entered into force on 5 January 2023. This affects approximately 50,000 European companies, including small and medium enterprises, and will require companies to report according to the European Sustainability Reporting Standards, developed by EFRAG, which provides the technical advice on reporting matters to the European Commission.

---

4 www.ion.icaew.com/ClientFiles/a42b9c80-6acd-4dca-980a-bac45d9a324d/MervynKingspeech. pdf, accessed 7 June 2014.
5 The provisions can be broken down as follows: 73 from Africa and Middle East, 174 from Asia Pacific, 245 from Europe, 37 from North America and 85 from South America (UNEP et al., 2020).

These standards are currently available as exposure drafts. They are cross-cutting and incorporate general requirements and disclosures, as well as topical reporting requirements, presented in terms of an ESG framework:

- Environment (E1 – E5): Climate change, Pollution, Water and marine resources, Biodiversity and ecosystems, Resources and circular economy
- Social (S1 – S4): Own workforce, Workers in the value chain, Affected communities, Customers and end-users
- Governance (G1): Business conduct

Over time, the requirements will be complemented by sector documents.

The business case for reporting

Corporate responsibility reporting is important because it is good for business and because it is the right thing to do. This is the classic argument of enlightened self-interest – doing well by doing good. As was described above, in the early years, companies reported on so-called non-financial matters in order to appease stakeholders who wanted more information and complained heavily if it was not provided. Many companies who did this type of reporting did so not because they thought that it was material to business performance but because they felt some moral obligation to do so or because they perceived a reputational risk if they did not.

Today there is growing consensus that stakeholders, not only shareholders, have a legitimate interest in obtaining material information about company performance. This includes environmental, social and governance (ESG) information. Some companies recognise the moral imperative to provide this information, based on the fundamental governance values of honesty, transparency and accountability.

However, currently the main driver for reporting is the business case. Material information on company performance has to focus on both financial and non-financial information. In terms of the correlation between responsible business and corporate performance, the work on *shared value* by Porter and Kramer has received significant attention, and in terms of integrated reporting, the work of Eccles has been very influential. For example, Eccles, Ionannou and Serafeim (The Impact of a Corporate Culture of Sustainability on Corporate Behavior and Performance, 2011) have demonstrated that what they call "high sustainability companies" significantly outperform their counterparts over the long term. Based on a detailed analysis of a sample of 180 companies, these authors state clearly that sustainable firms generate significantly higher profits and stock returns (Eccles et al., 2011: 30). In terms of the contributing factors that might provide this competitive advantage, they list a more engaged workforce, a more secure license to operate, a more loyal and satisfied customer base, better relationships with stakeholders, greater transparency, a more collaborative community and a better ability to innovate (Eccles et al., 2011: 30). They also highlight the importance of measurement and disclosure, stating:

> Reporting on performance measures, which are often non-financial regarding sustainability topics, to the board is an essential element of corporate governance, so that the board can form an opinion about whether management is executing the strategy of the organization well.
>
> (Eccles et al., 2011: 20)

By engaging in corporate responsibility reporting, companies benefit through improved understanding of the business model and better decision-making, increased investor confidence, improved reputation and stakeholder support. Integrated reporting emphasises the link between management information and external communication, as well as the need for integrated thinking.

In a global survey conducted by Chatham House, major stakeholder groups identified the following five issues as the greatest benefits of sustainability reporting: data transparency, organisational governance, reporting universe (getting more organisations to think about sustainable development issues), stakeholder engagemen and data comparability (Hohnen, 2012).

The main role players

The main role players in this field can be divided into three groups: those who want companies to report (sometimes, but not always, equivalent to the readers of reports), those who set the standards on what and how to report and – of course – the reporting companies themselves. We will call these groups users, standard setters and reporters, respectively. Report users include a very wide variety of stakeholders, including investors, local communities and advocacy groups. Ironically, one of the most powerful stakeholder groups in terms of influencing behaviour (namely investors) had been less interested in corporate responsibility reporting for decades. This position has changed as investors realise that ESG factors are becoming increasingly material to business success. The need for investors to have comparable and standardised data has been a major driver behind reporting standards. In an article that was published in the *Financial Times*, this point was highlighted by Michael Bloomberg and Mary Schapiro, at the time chairman and vice-chairman of the Sustainability Accounting Standards Board, who are quoted as saying: "Standardizing disclosure of sustainability information could bring significant financial benefits for shareholders and potential investors – and help strengthen the global economy's long-term health."[6]

---

6 www.ft.com/cms/s/0/0d9ccea6-db66-11e3-94ad-00144feabdc0.html#ixzz3450pIUC, accessed 8 June 2014.

From the investors' point of view, two of the most significant groups that can influence reporting practices are stock exchanges and institutional investors. The stock exchanges that have been most active in terms of reporting include those from South Africa and Brazil, while the FTSE4Good Index in the UK and the Dow Jones Sustainability Index in the US have also improved disclosure. In this regard the Sustainable Stock Exchanges Initiative is also of particular importance.

From an institutional investor perspective, two of the most important initiatives are the UN Principles for Responsible Investment (UN PRI) and the International Corporate Governance Network (ICGN). Although the collective efforts from these initiatives are important, the individual efforts of members or signatories are just as significant.

The standard-setting environment has become increasingly cluttered. In terms of reporting standards, until a few years ago the most important initiatives were the Global Reporting Initiative (GRI), the International Integrated Reporting Council (IIRC) and the Sustainability Accounting Standards Board (SASB). However, that has changed dramatically with the establishment of the International Sustainability Standards Board in 2021.

The Global Reporting Initiative

The Global Reporting Initiative (GRI) was the leader in the field in terms of reporting guidelines for sustainability reporting for many years. The mission of the GRI is to develop and disseminate globally applicable sustainability reporting guidelines for voluntary use by organisations reporting on the economic, environmental and social dimensions of their activities, products and services. This standard is important within the context of governance, since the elements of corporate social responsibility and sustainability are regarded as integral to sound corporate governance. The need to measure and report on any activity accurately is a key requirement for transparency, hence the importance of this standard. The GRI embraces the principles of transparency, inclusiveness, auditability, completeness, relevance, sustainability context, accuracy, neutrality, comparability, clarity and timeliness. In 2006 the GRI published its G3 Reporting Guidelines, comprising reporting principles; reporting guidance; a set of standard disclosures on strategy, company profile and management approach; and specific economic, social and environmental performance indicators. In May 2013 the GRI published its G4 Reporting Guidelines, describing the aim of G4 as follows: "to help reporters prepare sustainability reports that matter – and to make robust and purposeful sustainability reporting standard practice".[7]

---

7   www.globalreporting.org/resourcelibrary/GRI-An-introduction-to-G4.pdf, accessed 24 November 2014.

The field of corporate reporting is developing rapidly and has resulted in conceptual confusion between sustainability reporting, integrated reporting, non-financial reporting and environmental, social and governance (ESG) reporting. With a multitude of stakeholders (investors, regulators, civil society) all focusing on different aspects and highlighting different requirements, it has become a maze for both producers and consumers of corporate responsibility reports.

The GRI describes the link between sustainability reporting and integrated reporting as follows (Global Reporting Initiative, 2013: 85):

> Sustainability reporting is a process that assists organizations in setting goals, measuring performance and managing change towards a sustainable global economy – one that combines long term profitability with social responsibility and environmental care. Sustainability reporting – mainly through but not limited to a sustainability report – is the key platform for communicating the organization's economic, environmental, social and governance performance, reflecting positive and negative impacts. . . . Integrated reporting is an emerging and evolving trend in corporate reporting, which in general aims primarily to offer an organization's providers of financial capital with an integrated representation of the key factors that are material to its present and future value creation. Integrated reporters build on sustainability reporting foundations and disclosures in preparing their integrated report. Through the integrated report, an organization provides a concise communication about how its strategy, governance, performance and prospects lead to the creation of value over time. Therefore, the integrated report is not intended to be an extract of the traditional annual report nor a combination of the annual financial statements and the sustainability report.

There are different explanations for why the GRI did not participate in the recent global process of consolidation that is now driven by the International Sustainability Standards Board (ISSB). Perhaps there was some politics involved, but there is a clear difference in terms of the materiality focus of each side. The GRI embraces double materiality. In terms of this approach companies need to report not only on the impact of sustainability issues on its own performance but also its impact on society and the environment. The ISSB, in its attempt to develop a global baseline, is only focusing on single materiality, the impact of sustainability issues on the company. The GRI is an important stakeholder and has a lot to offer. Hopefully the after-the-fact agreement signed between the two parties will still result in something positive.

Integrated reporting

The concept of integrated reporting was first introduced by the GRI and, following extensive consultation amongst stakeholders, resulted in the establishment of the International Integrated Reporting Council (IRRC) in 2010. At the time, the thinking was that integrated reporting would result in the "merger" of financial and sustainability information and that – over time – both the annual financial report and the sustainability report would be replaced by one integrated report. That did not happen.

The IIRC defined an integrated report as "a concise communication about how an organization's strategy, governance, performance and prospects, in the context of its external environment, lead to the creation of value in the short, medium and long term".[8] The integrated report should not be confused with integrated *reporting*, which is defined as "a process founded on integrated thinking that results in a periodic integrated report by an organization about value creation over time and related communications regarding aspects of value creation".[9]

During the early days of conceptual clarification about integrated reporting, *Making Investment Grade: the Future of Corporate Reporting* (Van der Lugt & Malan, 2012) brought together the views of some early pioneers in the field. In the introduction, the editors explain that reporting preferences are often presented as opposites, but that the developments in terms of integration point to more suitable midways. Examples of opposites are: (Van der Lugt & Malan, 2012: 8):

[Q]uantitative versus qualitative information, core indicators versus additional indicators, historical information versus forward-looking information, input indicators versus output indicators, process indicators versus performance indicators, physical metrics versus financial metrics, micro level, local site versus macro level, aggregated data, tangible versus intangible asset values, internal (private) versus external (public) information, and direct versus indirect impact or dependence.

In the case of financial reporting, investors and regulators drive reporting. In the case of sustainability reporting, there is a wider range of interest groups, including sustainability experts, consultants, data compilers, researchers and rating agencies. Internally, key drivers are those with a special interest in finance or sustainability, as well as those tasked with the responsibility of overseeing and leading the process of reporting. The role of the board is also important. Because there are so many silos in most organisations, the creation of reporting integration teams is recommended.

As it turned out, the question whether reporting process should lead to the publication of one or multiple reports was the wrong question. The editors argued that it is more useful to think in terms of a pyramid of communication

8 www.theiirc.org, accessed 5 April 2014.
9 www.theiirc.org, accessed 5 April 2014.

tools with a concise integrated report at the top, followed by a second layer of financial and sustainability data, as well as further layers that target specific audiences.

The following statement is noteworthy: "The reporting pyramid also signals the importance for the integrated report at the top, to be not simply an object that displays superficially condensed information but really something that reflects a deeper quality information" (Van der Lugt & Malan, 2012: 130).

Determining materiality is not a simple, mechanistic decision. A more inclusive understanding of materiality, as opposed to the definition used in financial reporting, refers to the ability to make a judgement regarding the capacity of an organisation to create and sustain value.

The dominant assumption is that investors are the main target audience for integrated reporting. Regulation will be a key determinant of content and therefore also of the audience. If the integrated report becomes a legal document filled with disclaimers, it will lose its value not only for investors but also for other potential readers of the report.

Ultimately the board of directors has to govern the process of integrated reporting. Shareholder activism and more active engagement of citizens as providers of capital through pension funds will broaden the governance base.

Questions about regulation address the fundamental issue of the correct balance between mandatory requirements and market-driven innovation. The risk of excessive regulation is that it will lead to mindless, quantitative compliance. There are some early examples of innovative, hybrid systems combining smart regulation and self-regulation. Figure 6.2, developed by Van der Lugt, illustrates that the integrated report has to fill a space that neither sustainability reporting nor annual financial reporting has been able to capture effectively.

The International Sustainability Standards Board

The establishment of the International Sustainability Standards Board (ISSB) was announced by the IFRS Foundation on 3 November 2021 at COP26 in Glasgow. The IFRS Foundation oversees the International Accounting Standards Board (IASB) which sets the accounting standards in more than 140 jurisdictions around the world. This explains the significance of the ISSB – in a very short period of time established itself as the core of the sustainability standards industry. Some of the organisations that paved the way for the creation of the ISSB are the International Organization for Securities Commissions (IOSCO), the Climate Disclosure Standards Board (CDSB), the IASB, the Task Force for Climate-related Disclosures (TCFD), the Value Reporting Foundation (VRF – which brought together the Integrated Reporting Framework and SASB Standards) and the World Economic Forum (WEF).

The ISSB makes it clear that it is building on the work of investor-focused reporting initiatives, for example, the Climate Disclosure Standards Board,

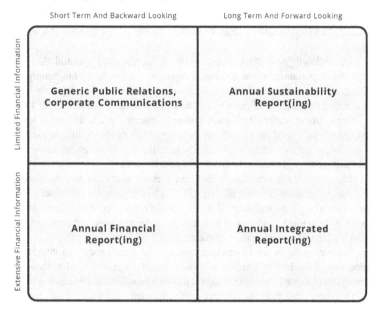

Figure 6.2 Positioning the integrated report

Source: Van der Lugt & Malan (2012: 134)

the Task Force for Climate-related Financial Disclosures (TCFD), the Value Reporting and the World Economic Forum's Stakeholder Capitalism Metrics. The ISSB encourages companies to use these frameworks until new standards are available, and does not mention the GRI at all.

In May 2023 there were two draft disclosure standards available: general sustainability-related disclosures and climate-related disclosures. The stated intention of the ISSB is "to deliver a comprehensive global baseline of sustainability-related disclosure standards that provide investors and other capital market participants with information about companies' sustainability-related risks and opportunities to help them make informed decisions".[10]

It is clear that there will continue to be rapid development and further consolidation in the reporting space. Europe is leading in terms of regulation. I have already mentioned the Corporate Sustainability Reporting Directive, which has made it compulsory for companies to disclose information on the social and environmental impact of their own operations and also within their value chain.

10 www.ifrs.org/groups/international-sustainability-standards-board/.

From a global perspective, it is anticipated that the ISSB will become the single point of reference for sustainability reporting and that governments and regulators will increasingly incorporate these standards into mandatory reporting requirements.

References

Eccles, B., Ioannou, I. & Serafeim, G. 2011. *The impact of a corporate culture of sustainability on corporate behavior and performance*. Working paper no. 12–035. Boston: Harvard Business School.

Global Reporting Initiative. 2013. *G4 Sustainability reporting guidelines*. [Online] Available: www.globalreporting.org/resourcelibrary/GRIG4-Part1-Reporting-Principles-and-Standard-Disclosures.pdf Accessed: 28 November 2014.

KPMG International. 2022. KPMG international survey of corporate responsibility reporting 2022. [Online] Available: https://assets.kpmg/content/dam/kpmg/xx/pdf/2022/10/ssr-small-steps-big-shifts.pdf.

OECD. 2011. *OECD guidelines for multinational enterprises*. [Online] Available: http://mneguidelines.oecd.org/text/ Accessed: 14 June 2015.

Smith, K. & Alexander, J. 2013. Which CSR-related headings do fortune 500 companies use on their websites.[question mark] *Business Communication Quarterly*, 76(2), 155–171.

UNEP; GRI, University of Stellenbosch Business School. 2020. *Carrots and sticks – sustainability reporting policy: Global trends in disclosure as the ESG agenda goes mainstream*. [Online] Available: www.carrotsandsticks.net.

UNEP, KPMG, GRI & Centre for Corporate Governance in Africa. 2013. *Sustainability reporting policies worldwide – today's best practice, tomorrow's trends*. [Online] Available: www.governance.usb.ac.za/pdfs/Carrots-and-Sticks.pdf Accessed: 14 June 2015.

Van der Lugt, C. & Malan, D. (eds.). 2012. *Making investment grade: The future of corporate reporting*. Cape Town: United Nations Environment Programme, Deloitte, Centre for Corporate Governance in Africa (University of Stellenbosch Business School).

7   Regulating responsibility

He who was so unjust as to do his brother an injury will scarce be so just as to condemn himself for it.

John Locke

Written laws are like spiders' webs; they will catch, it is true, the weak and poor, but would be torn in pieces by the rich and powerful.

Anacharsis – sixth century BC

Voluntary versus mandatory standards

From a corporate perspective, regulation is usually viewed through a compliance lens. Sometimes regulation with regards to corporate responsibility is mandatory, for example the anti-bribery or human rights legislation. But with corporate responsibility, more often than not, the regulations are voluntary, for example the UN Global Compact or various ISO standards.

With reference to the future regulation of the principles contained in the UN Global Compact, Rasche (2010) states that it would be naive to believe that corporate responsibility should remain entirely voluntary. He suggests that the knowledge on social and environmental issues affects corporations and could be used to improve legislation throughout the world. This, according to him, will be a necessary next step to achieve the ambitious goals of the UN Global Compact (Rasche, 2010: 2).

Leisinger (2007: 4) makes the distinction between legitimacy and legality: "reliance on law alone triggers legalistic, compliance-based attitudes and, where the quality of law is inadequate, entails vulnerabilities even for corporations acting legally. Legitimate corporate conduct, by contrast, is being seen to do the right thing beyond legal minima."

McIntosh and Waddock (2010: 230) argue that progressive corporations around the world that align their practices with the values of the UN Global Compact have already gone beyond existing regulation and therefore are

DOI: 10.4324/9781003356981-7

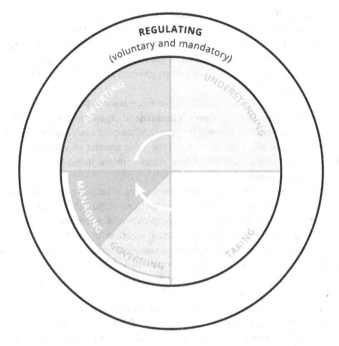

Figure 7.1 Regulating responsibility

setting new standards. They suggest that the playing field has to be levelled at some stage and therefore that new regulation will be required. The authors make a significant point about the historical roots of the UN Global Compact:

> Governments, after all, were the original signatories to the treaties from which the Global Compact's Principles derive, and they probably eventually will need to take a stronger role in enforcing these types of standards, particularly to deal with the numerous laggards who are not already up to speed with the types of changes needed.

Since the crisis of 2008 there has been a shift in corporate views on the role of government in the economy. It is difficult to point fingers at government and accept a bailout at the same time. Today the need for strong government intervention is acknowledged by many. In the 2013 *UN Global Compact – Accenture CEO Study on Sustainability*, there is acknowledgement that large corporations cannot address current challenges on its own (UN Global Compact and Accenture, 2013). According to Peter Lacy from Accenture, the study suggests that "business may collectively have reached a plateau in the advancement of sustainability. Without radical, structural changes to markets and systems, CEOs believe, business may be unable to lead the way toward the peak of a sustainable economy" (UN Global Compact and Accenture, 2013: 5). For example, 85 per cent of CEOs surveyed in the study demand clearer policies and market signals from governments (UN Global Compact and Accenture, 2013: 13).

Governments have to regulate and enforce laws in the domestic sphere, but also coordinate globally through multilateral organisations to ensure that appropriate, compatible, fair and flexible regulations are in place across country borders. This will include the need for a fair amount of voluntary guidelines but – given the number of free riders – might increasingly focus on mandatory requirements.

Investors and other stakeholders should keep a keen eye on both governments and corporations and encourage them to act responsibly. Of course, this is easier said than done. We live in a complex world where the lines between the public and private domains are blurred, where short-term expectations of voters or shareholders are often decisive and where each individual decision-maker is driven by the very human reality of looking after his or her own interests. In the famous words of Upton Sinclair: "It is difficult to get a man to understand something when his salary depends on his not understanding it."[1]

Clearly there is a sense of urgency and a real risk that impatience will result in violence and disruption. Assertions about the supremacy of capital markets will increasingly evoke the image of a violin playing with smoke in the background. Even with increasing demands for rapid change, the realistic view is that progress will be incremental. The well-known historian Tony Judt was pragmatic in his advice on how to tackle the big issues of the twenty-first century (Judt, 2010: 224):

> We need to apologize a little less for past shortcomings and speak more assertively of achievements. That these were always incomplete should not trouble us. If we have learned nothing else from the 20th century, we should at least have grasped that the more perfect the answer, the more terrifying its consequences. Incremental improvements upon unsatisfactory circumstances are the best that we can hope for, and probably all we should seek.

The debate about the correct balance – or choice – between voluntary and mandatory standards is a complex one that spans a wide variety of areas. In terms of sustainability reporting, research conducted by KPMG, UNEP, the GRI and the Unit for Corporate Governance (KPMG et al., 2010: 4) highlights

---

1 www.goodreads.com/author/quotes/23510.Upton_Sinclair, accessed 21 December 2014.

the following trends in terms of the general area of corporate responsibility regulation:

- Acknowledgement of the need for a more active role for the state to ensure risk prevention and disclosure.
- An emphasis on complementarity, that is, a balance between voluntary and mandatory standards.
- A focus on the integration of governance, financial and sustainability issues.

Regulation of corporate responsibility can focus on either performance or disclosure (or both). If the focus is on performance, the regulator will focus on specific compliance standards, for example, the legal minimum wage, minimum employment age, levels of greenhouse gas emissions, etc. If the focus is on disclosure, there will be a specific requirement to disclose, either to the regulator or stakeholders in general, how the company performed (not necessarily in terms of compliance). Examples include compulsory disclosure of executive remuneration or time lost owing to work-related injuries. These areas are not mutually exclusive, and in many cases there can be strict performance as well as disclosure requirements.

One of the interesting balancing acts between a mandatory and voluntary approach is the "comply or explain" principle. Essentially this approach forms a hybrid between the different approaches as well as the focus areas. "Comply or explain" is mandatory but leaves discretionary powers to the organisation to provide reasons for the cases where it decided not to comply. It also bridges the divide between performance and disclosure, because the compliance aspect is linked to actual performance, and the explanation (in the case of non-compliance) is a disclosure requirement.

Because of the lack of a global regulator, most of the global standards tend to be voluntary, such as the UN Global Compact. Some of the other voluntary standards that have already been discussed include the Global Reporting Initiative, the UN Principles for Responsible Investment and various governance codes, such as King III and the UK Corporate Governance Code. In addition, there are standards such as the International Organization for Standardization (ISO) 26000 Standard on Corporate Responsibility, the OECD Guidelines for Multinational Enterprises, the Millennium Development Goals (MDGs) and their replacement, the Sustainable Development Goals (SDGs). There are also the CERES Principles, SA 8000 and AA1000, but these will not be discussed in detail here because they are not presently as influential as the others.

All these initiatives are characterised by the fact that they are voluntary – this includes the SDGs from a corporate perspective (i.e. corporations may voluntarily adopt one or more of the SDGs) as opposed to the position of governments that have ratified these goals formally. Voluntarism is often used as a criticism against such initiatives, but such criticism fails to acknowledge the specific role these initiatives play within society.

For example, in 2008 a coalition of civil society organisations attacked the UN Global Compact because they argued that one of its signatories (Petrochina) was involved in human rights abuses. The specific context was Petrochina's involvement in the Darfur region of Sudan.

At the time, Bart Slob from the Amsterdam-based Centre of Research on Multinational Corporations stated: "Without any effective monitoring and enforcement provisions, the UN Global Compact fails to hold corporations accountable."[2] This accusation misses the point that the UN Global Compact was not created as an enforcement mechanism.[3] Just as Transparency International will not take countries to the International Court of Justice even if they find convincing evidence of grand corruption, it is not the role of the UN Global Compact actively to police compliance with its principles. In the same way, the Global Reporting Initiative is not required to prevent tobacco corporations or nuclear arms manufacturers from issuing sustainability reports. To be fair, the UN Global Compact does reserve the right to delist companies if there is evidence of "systematic or egregious abuse of the UN Global Compact's overall aims and principles", and if such companies do not respond to requests for engagement. The Petrochina case was the first real challenge for the Compact in this regard, and the board of directors ultimately decided not to act against Petrochina.

The response was that it would not act because "[the UN Global Compact] is not a mediation, dispute resolution or adjudicative body, nor is it an enforcement agency".[4] It remains to be seen what will happen if a company is delisted for any reason other than non-communication, the most objective criterion that could be applied. It is possible that the floodgates will open in terms of NGOs and pressure groups accusing UN Global Compact signatories of misdemeanours. This is exactly what the UN Global Compact would like to prevent, and certainly it does not have the capacity to cope with such demands. It is interesting to note the UN Global Compact's position in terms of tobacco corporations:[5]

> The UN Global Compact Office supports the World Health Organization's efforts to raise awareness of the serious health effects of tobacco use. It thus actively discourages tobacco companies from participation in the initiative and does not accept funding from tobacco companies. It also does

2 Press release by Investors Against Genocide and Act for Darfur, 12 May 2008.
3 The Global Compact reserves the right to engage with companies if there is evidence of "systematic or egregious abuse of the Global Compact's overall aims and principles". However, in this case the strongest sanction remains to list a company as non-communicative and ultimately to delist it if it does not respond to requests for information on the accusations of abuse.
4 See www.triplepundit.com/story/2008/petrochina-plea-turned-down/98841.
5 www.unglobalcompact.org/HowToParticipate/Business_Participation/tobacco_company_policy.html, accessed 18 December 2014 (link no longer active).

Table 7.1 Comparison between main categories of international standards

UN Global Compact	MDGs	SDGs	ISO 26000	OECD Guidelines
Protection of internationally proclaimed human rights	Eradicate extreme poverty and hunger	No poverty	Organisational governance	Concepts and principles
Non-complicity in human rights abuses	Achieve universal primary education	Zero hunger	Human rights	General policies
Freedom of association and right to collective bargaining	Promote gender equality and empower women	Good health and well-being	Labour practices	Disclosure
Elimination of forced and compulsory labour	Reduce child mortality	Quality education	The environment	Employment and industrial relations
Abolition of child labour	Improve maternal health	Gender equality	Fair operating practices	Environment
Elimination of discrimination	Combat HIV/AIDS, malaria and other diseases	Clean water and sanitation	Consumer issues	Combatting bribery
Precautionary approach to environmental challenges	Ensure environmental sustainability	Affordable and clean energy	Community involvement and development	Consumer interests
Environmental responsibility initiatives	Develop a Global Partnership for Development	Decent work and economic growth		Science and technology
Development and diffusion of environmentally friendly technologies		Industry, innovation and infrastructure		Competition
Work against corruption, including extortion and bribery		Reduced inequalities		Taxation
		Sustainable cities and communities		
		Responsible consumption and production		
		Climate action		
		Life below water		
		Life on land		
		Peace, justice and strong institutions		
		Partnerships for the goals		

not permit tobacco companies to make presentations at any of its global events or to use the global brand in any other way to raise their profile. Since tobacco is a legal product whose use UN Member States have not yet outlawed, the Global Compact Office is not able to exclude tobacco companies from the initiative if they still wish to join. . . . Until Member States decide otherwise, tobacco companies should not be immune from the Global Compact's worldwide call to all companies to embrace, support and enact within their sphere of influence the set of core values in these areas. They should be expected to support and respect human rights, uphold labour standards, respect the environment and avoid corruption.

Table 7.2 compares the main categories of a few selected standards, including the predecessor of the Sustainable Development Goals (SDGs), the Millennium Development Goals (MDGs). There is some overlap in terms of focus areas for the UN Global Compact, ISO 26000 and the OECD Guidelines, as well as a more specific focus on human rights elements from the MDGs. Given that the MDGs were first and foremost a governmental initiative, this is to be expected. The following section will introduce these selected standards in further detail.

Table 7.2 Millenium Development Goals compared to Sustainable Development Goals

Millenium Development Goals	Sustainable Development Goals (rearranged))
Eradicate extreme poverty and hunger.	• End poverty in all its forms everywhere. • End hunger, achieve food security and improved nutrition and promote sustainable agriculture. • Reduce inequality within and among countries.
Achieve universal primary education.	• Ensure inclusive and equitable quality education and promote lifelong learning opportunities for all.
Promote gender equality and empower women.	• Achieve gender equality and empower all women and girls.
Reduce child mortality.	• Ensure healthy lives and promote well-being for all at all ages.
Improve maternal health.	
Combat HIV/Aids, malaria and other diseases.	
Ensure environmental sustainability.	• Ensure availability and sustainable management of water and sanitation for all. • Ensure access to affordable, reliable, sustainable and modern energy for all.

Millenium Development Goals	Sustainable Development Goals (rearranged))
	• Make cities and human settlements inclusive, safe, resilient and sustainable. • Ensure sustainable consumption and production patterns. • Take urgent action to combat climate change and its impacts. • Conserve and sustainably use the oceans, seas and marine resources for sustainable development. • Protect, restore and promote sustainable use of terrestrial ecosystems, sustainably manage forests, combat desertification, halt and reverse land degradation and halt biodiversity loss.
Develop a Global Partnership for Development.	• Promote sustained, inclusive and sustainable economic growth, full and productive employment and decent work for all. • Build resilient infrastructure, promote inclusive and sustainable industrialisation and foster innovation. • Promote peaceful and inclusive societies for sustainable development, provide access to justice for all and build effective, accountable and inclusive institutions at all levels. • Strengthen the means of implementation, and revitalise the global partnership for sustainable development.

The Millennium Development Goals

Although no longer applicable, from a historical perspective it is still important to take cognisance of the UN Millennium Development Goals (MDGs). The MDGs were signed off by governments in 2000 and are listed below:

• Eradicate extreme poverty and hunger.
• Achieve universal primary education.
• Promote gender equality and empower women.
• Reduce child mortality.
• Improve maternal health.
• Combat HIV/Aids, malaria and other diseases.
• Ensure environmental sustainability.
• Develop a global partnership for development.

The Sustainable Development Goals

At the Rio+20 conference it was agreed by member states to launch the development of a set of Sustainable Development Goals (SDGs). The intention was that the SDGs should build on the MDGs and also converge with the post-2015 development agenda. This agenda has been driven by a group of eminent persons appointed by the UN secretary general. In a report, *High-Level Panel of Eminent Persons on the post-2015 Development Agenda*, 2013, the group suggested the following five transformative shifts:

- Leave no one behind.
- Put sustainable development at the core.
- Transform economies for jobs and inclusive growth.
- Build peace and effective, open and accountable institutions for all.
- Forge a new global partnership.

The intergovernmental Open Working Group was created, and it submitted a report with proposals to the 68th session of the UN General Assembly in 2013. The proposal of the Open Working Group (2014: 6) was that there should be 17 new Sustainable Development Goals, namely:

1. End poverty in all its forms everywhere.
2. End hunger, achieve food security and improved nutrition and promote sustainable agriculture.
3. Ensure healthy lives and promote well-being for all at all ages.
4. Ensure inclusive and equitable quality education and promote lifelong learning opportunities for all.
5. Achieve gender equality and empower all women and girls.
6. Ensure availability and sustainable management of water and sanitation for all.
7. Ensure access to affordable, reliable, sustainable and modern energy for all.
8. Promote sustained, inclusive and sustainable economic growth, full and productive employment and decent work for all.
9. Build resilient infrastructure, promote inclusive and sustainable industrialisation and foster innovation.
10. Reduce inequality within and among countries.
11. Make cities and human settlements inclusive, safe, resilient and sustainable.
12. Ensure sustainable consumption and production patterns.
13. Take urgent action to combat climate change and its impacts.
14. Conserve and sustainably use the oceans, seas and marine resources for sustainable development.

15. Protect, restore and promote sustainable use of terrestrial ecosystems, sustainably manage forests, combat desertification, halt and reverse land degradation, and halt biodiversity loss.
16. Promote peaceful and inclusive societies for sustainable development, provide access to justice for all, and build effective, accountable and inclusive institutions at all levels.
17. Strengthen the means of implementation and revitalise the global partnership for sustainable development.

The SDGs were formally approved at a UN Summit in September 2015 and came into force on 1 January 2016.

Table 7.3 compares the MDGs to the proposed SDGs. It is noteworthy that the most comprehensive expansion has been in the area of environmental sustainability, while previous goals relating to health and child mortality have been consolidated into one goal to "ensure healthy lives and promote well-being for all at all ages". The use of the word "revitalise" with regard to the global partnership is significant. There seems to be implicit acknowledgement that this partnership has not been as effective as it could have been. Again, there are additional goals that provide more substance to this goal: specific reference is made to issues such as economic growth, employment and industrialisation, while the ethical principles of justice, accountability and inclusivity are also made explicit.

Figure 7.2 displays the iconic SDG infographic. It is hard to believe that we have already passed the halfway mark on the road to 2030!

Figure 7.2 The official SDG infographic

Source: United Nations

The ISO 26000 standard

The International Organization for Standardization (ISO) is an independent, non-governmental membership organisation based in Geneva, Switzerland. ISO is the largest developer of voluntary international standards in the world and is made up of the national standards bodies from 165 member countries.[6]

In 2010 the ISO launched its standard on social responsibility. ISO 26000:2010 is not a certifiable standard but provides guidance on the concept of social responsibility. Its aim is to help organisations regardless of their activity, size or location. The launch followed a five-year period of intensive stakeholder engagement, involving governments, industry representatives, consumer groups and labour organisations. The standard is not publicly available but is sold for CHF208 (approximately €200) by the ISO. Figure 7.3 provides a schematic overview of ISO 26000.

ISO 26 000 provides guidance on the following aspects:[7]

- Concepts, terms and definitions related to social responsibility.
- The background, trends and characteristics of social responsibility.
- Principles and practices relating to social responsibility.
- The core subjects and issues of social responsibility.
- Integrating, implementing and promoting socially responsible behaviour throughout the organisation and, through its policies and practices, within its sphere of influence.
- Identifying and engaging with stakeholders.
- Communicating commitments, performance and other information related to social responsibility.

The following recommendation of the ISO seems to be in line with the ISCT requirement of moral free space:[8]

> In applying ISO 26000:2010, it is advisable that an organization take into consideration societal, environmental, legal, cultural, political and organizational diversity, as well as differences in economic conditions, while being consistent with international norms of behaviour.

It is difficult to gauge the usage of ISO 26000 among corporations. At a meeting that was convened by ISO in 2012, it was mentioned that a Google search

---

6 More information is available at www.iso.org.
7 www.iso.org/iso/home/store/catalogue_tc/catalogue_detail.htm?csnumber=42546, accessed 24 November 2014.
8 www.iso.org/iso/home/store/catalogue_tc/catalogue_detail.htm?csnumber=42546, accessed 24 November 2014.

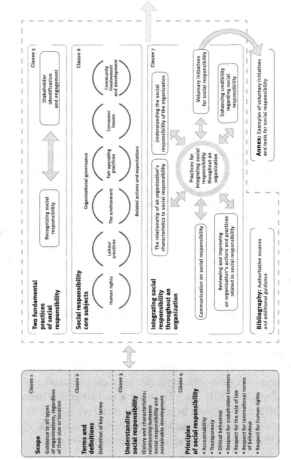

Figure 7.3 Schematic overview of ISO 26000

Source: www.iso.org

returned two million hits,[9] but there was no mention of the number of companies actually using it.

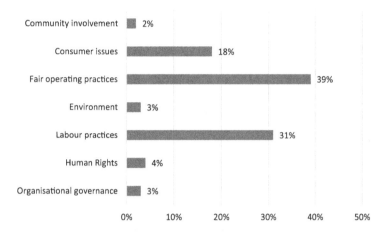

Figure 7.4 Dilemmas mapped against ISO 26000 categories

Figure 7.4 presents the mapping of the same dilemmas used before, this time mapped against the seven core subjects of the ISO 26000 standard. Fair operating practices (which include corruption issues) remain the most relevant category from an individual ethical dilemma perspective. The more detailed structure of the ISO 26000 standard enables a more sophisticated understanding of individual ethical dilemmas. Labour practices also feature significantly, while the more specialised areas (human rights and environment) do not result in many dilemmas at the individual level.

OECD Guidelines for Multinational Enterprises

The Organisation for Economic Cooperation and Development (OECD) Guidelines for Multinational Enterprises (the Guidelines) provide "non-binding principles and standards for responsible business conduct in a global context consistent with applicable laws and internationally recognised standards" (OECD, 2011: 3).[10] The current version of the Guidelines was released in 2011 and endorsed by all OECD members as well as Argentina, Brazil, Egypt, Latvia, Lithuania, Morocco, Peru and Romania. The original version was launched in 1976 and has been reviewed five times.

---

9 www.iso.org/iso/home/news_index/news_archive/news.htm?refid=Ref1691, accessed 24 November 2014.
10 For background information on the OECD, visit www.oecd.org.

The Guidelines provide voluntary principles and standards for responsible business conduct in the following areas: human rights, employment and industrial relations, environment, combating bribery, bribe solicitation and extortion, consumer interests, science and technology and competition. A general set of policies contained in the Guidelines has been included in Appendix E.

In concluding the discussion on regulation, it needs to be admitted that this section has barely scratched the surface in terms of the plethora of both voluntary and mandatory standards and regulations available worldwide. Compliance with mandatory standards will always be the starting point, and it will only be in the rarest of circumstances – where an argument can be made for moral obligation – to disregard mandatory standards. Repudiating a mandatory standard would be the corporate equivalent of civil disobedience but would be applicable in cases where the legal framework itself is morally unacceptable, for example the laws that existed under Apartheid South Africa. From a human rights perspective, this argument also applies for corporations operating in countries where human rights are not systematically protected.

In terms of voluntary standards, corporations need to make a selection based on alignment with their own values, regional and industry requirements, as well as the interest and demands of stakeholders. The UN Global Compact is the world's largest initiative in this space, but that does not mean that corporations should therefore automatically jump on this bandwagon. On the contrary, it has been shown that participation in the initiative brings with it huge responsibilities, and to safeguard the reputation of the initiative itself as well as that of participants, the decision to participate should not be taken lightly.

The B20 process

During 2022, I had the privilege of acting as one of the co-chairs of the Business 20 (B20) task force on Integrity and Compliance. The B20 is the official business voice that communicates with the G20. It was established in 2010 and formulates and presents policy recommendations on designated issues to the G20 on an annual basis. The B20 has a number of task forces, including the Integrity and Compliance Task Force. Others include trade and investment, energy, sustainability & climate, digitalization, finance & infrastructure, future of work & education as well as a woman in business action council.

The B20 Task Force on Integrity and Compliance comprises representatives from the international business community and has a number of network partners, including the Basel Institute on Governance, Business at OECD, International Chamber of Commerce, IFAC, the Institute of Internal Auditors and the World Economic Forum. Examples of companies that are represented on the task force are Deloitte, Google, GSK, Mastercard, Novartis, Siemens and the World Bank Group. While the activities of the task force are not exactly the same from year to year, the typical process is to prepare a document with policy recommendations, developed through a consultative process, that is then submitted for inclusion in the overall B20 document and eventually presented to the G20 as part of the formal B20 Communique.

The core recommendations of the most recent Integrity and Compliance task force focused on sustainable governance to support ESG initiatives, collective action to alleviate integrity risks and measures to address risks associated with money laundering, terrorist financing and cybercrime (Business 20, 2022). The recommendations are summarised in the table below.

Table 7.3 The B20 task force recommendations

Recommendation	Policy actions
Promote sustainable governance[11] in business to support ESG initiatives	• Improve sustainable governance measures • Optimise sustainable governance compliance disclosures and monitoring
Foster collective action to alleviate integrity risks	• Cultivate and strengthen integrity through business-to-business collaboration • Facilitate integrity in business-to-government interactions • Promote inclusiveness between public-private sector entities to ensure trust, transparency and high standards of integrity • Promote inclusiveness between public-private sector entities to ensure trust, transparency and high standards of integrity
Foster agility in counteract measures to combat money laundering/ terrorist financing risks	• Refocus on money laundering/terrorist financing risk factors identification • Improve beneficial ownership transparency
Strengthen governance to mitigate exacerbated cybercrime risks	• Rectify organisational governance structure • Extend multi-stakeholder cooperation for better cybercrime response

Regulation will continue to play an important role in the development of corporate responsibility. Almost always, companies will face a hybrid of voluntary and mandatory standards. But as we have seen in the specific field of reporting, the trend is certainly in the direction of mandatory standards.

References

Business 20. 2022. *Integrity and compliance task force policy paper*. [Online] Available https://b20indonesia2022.org/view-doc-b20/policy_paper/MVY26ELP.
Judt, T. 2010. *Ill fares the land*. London: Penguin Books.

---

11 Sustainable governance is an evasive concept. Sometimes it seems to refer to the need for governance (the system by which organisations are directed and controlled in terms of the classic Cadbury definition) to focus extensively on sustainability issues, while at other times it is used to refer to the durability of governance itself.

KPMG; UNEP; GRI, Unit for Corporate Governance in Africa. 2010. *Carrots and sticks – Promoting transparency and sustainability: An update on trends in voluntary and mandatory approaches to sustainability reporting*. Amsterdam: Global Reporting Initiative.

Leisinger, K. 2007. Capitalism with a human face: The UN global compact. *Journal of Corporate Citizenship*, 28, 1–20.

McIntosh, M. & Waddock, S. 2010b. *The UN global compact: Looking forward ten years after*. [Online] Available: www.griffith.edu.au/business-commerce/sustainable-enterprise/resources/the-un-global-compact-looking-forward-ten-years-after Accessed: 28 October 2010.

OECD. 2011. *OECD guidelines for multinational enterprises*. [Online] Available: http://mneguidelines.oecd.org/text/ Accessed: 14 June 2015.

Open Working Group of the General Assembly on Sustainable Development Goals. 2014. *Open Working Group proposal for sustainable development goals*. United Nations, New York.

Rasche, A. 2010. *The UN global compact – a critique of its critiques*. [Online] Available: www.griffith.edu.au/business-commerce/sustainable-enterprise/resources/the-un-global-compact-looking-forward-ten-years-after Accessed: 28 October 2010.

UN Global Compact and Accenture. 2013. *The UN global compact-accenture CEO study on sustainability*. New York: United Nations Global Compact.

8 Conclusion

Johan de Witt, represented by the threatened swan in Asselijn's painting which was discussed in the introduction, died in 1672, twenty years after his appointment as the most powerful public servant in Holland. In that year, both England and France attacked Holland at the same time, and an angry mob in The Hague killed both Johan and his brother Cornelius in a gruesome fashion, as depicted in a painting by an unknown painter (Figure 8.1):[1]

Ironically, Asselijn's swan was not killed by the dog but by those whose interests the swan was supposed to protect, namely the hatchlings from the eggs in the painting. In a further historical twist, the swan became the aggressor at the expense of the dog. Holland invaded England in 1688, and Prince William of Orange became the King of England in April 1689 and was affectionately known to some as "King Billy".[2]

It is my hope that the future of corporate responsibility is more promising! We are indeed faced by many challenges, including geopolitical conflict, social inequality and climate change. The spectre of a violent and wounded world that is turned upside down sometimes seems too close for comfort. But in the context of this book, the threatened swan from the introduction can survive, thrive and prosper.

A conceptual framework was presented in this book, with the aim to advance thinking on how to conceptualise, develop and implement effective corporate responsibility programmes. The framework outlined, in sequence, the dimensions of understanding, taking, governing, managing, reporting on and regulating responsibility. This framework was developed with Donaldson and Dunfee's ISCT container as a major reference point and is therefore fully aligned with the core normative elements of ISCT. Examples include the acceptance of hypernorms to fully understand responsibility, active

---

1 For a more detailed description of this event, view www.rijksmuseum.nl/aria/aria_assets/ SK-A-15?lang=en& context_space=aria_encyclopedia&context_id=00047624, accessed 15 October 2010.
2 http://en.wikipedia.org/wiki/William_III_of_England, accessed 5 December 2014.

DOI: 10.4324/9781003356981-8

Figure 8.1 The bodies of the De Witt brothers, hanged at Groene Zoodje on Vijverberg
     in The Hague

Source: Courtesy of Rijksmuseum Amsterdam

engagement with moral free space when taking responsibility to make sense
at a local level, the development of micro contracts in the governance and
management of responsibility and applying integration in the activity of
reporting. Finally, it was demonstrated how international treaties are based on
hypernorms and how local legislation and other standards could be interpreted
as micro contracts. There is one more similarity between the entire framework and ISCT, and that can be described by the word "integrative". The
framework contains a normative component (understanding responsibility

and, to some degree, taking responsibility), as well as empirical components (governing, managing and reporting on responsibility). The empirical parts on their own are not sufficient, because they can only be captured in a descriptive way. They become more meaningful if they are framed by the normative components.

From a governance perspective, the framework is also aligned with the core governance principles of honesty (understanding and taking responsibility), accountability (governing and managing responsibility) and transparency (reporting on responsibility).

It was argued that the framework brings the evasive components of theory and practice a little closer to each other and also supports the project to end the methodological stand-off between the normative and empirical camps in business ethics theory. This is an area where Tom Donaldson has made a huge contribution, and I have no doubt that he is going to pursue this quest for the holy grail.

With each of these required activities, things can, and do, go wrong. Insincere chief executives can produce lofty statements of intent while doing the exact opposite; poor governance practices can reduce accountability and impede performance; poor management can result in ineffective action or complete lack thereof; and poor reporting practices can reduce transparency and impact negatively on reputation.

The framework proposed in this book guides action in every dimension of corporate responsibility. It is not a once-off, grand solution that will guarantee success. However, it does bring the evasive components of theory and practice a little closer to each other, and it provides additional backup for the broader project started by Donaldson and Dunfee.

The reality is that these divisions run deep and will continue to do so for some time. If the transition from "is" to "ought" remains methodologically elusive, perhaps a pragmatic compromise would be to derive a "could" from an "is". Something that "could be" is based on possibility and does not necessarily have to be grounded in either a moral case or a business case. It is aspirational and might be a much more effective rallying cry to inspire corporations and other stakeholders. It is in line with Freeman's (2002: 44) description of stakeholder theory as "a genre of stories about how we could live". There is remarkable consensus today about what is wrong with the "is". But to dream about what could be requires clarity of purpose. Shared dreams can be very powerful, and shared stories about successes achieved can act as inspiration, as long as they lead to action.

Prosperity is what the world needs, and given their power and a clear understanding of purpose, corporations around the globe – both big and small, listed or unlisted, privately or publicly owned, can make a huge contribution in this regard.

Bibliography

Barclays plc. 2013. *Citizenship plan*. London: Barclays plc.

Boatright, J. 2000. Contract theory and business ethics: A review of "ties that bind". *Business and Society Review*, 105(4), 452–466.

Bremer, J. 2008. How global is the global compact? *Business Ethics: A European Review*, 17(3), 227–244.

Brown, M. & Treviño, L. 2006. Ethical leadership: A review and future directions. *The Leadership Quarterly*, 17(2006), 595–616.

Bunnin, N. & Yu, J. 2004. *The Blackwell dictionary of western philosophy*. Malden, MA: Blackwell Publishing.

Business 20. 2022. *Integrity and compliance task force policy paper*. [Online] Available: https://b20indonesia2022.org/view-doc-b20/policy_paper/MVY26ELP.

Button, M.E. 2008. *Contract, culture and citizenship: Transformative liberalism from hobbes to rawls*. Philadelphia: Pennsylvania State University.

Carroll, A. 1999. Corporate social responsibility: Evolution of a definitional construct. *Business in Society*, 38(3), 268–295.

Carroll, A. & Buchholtz, A. 2006. *Business & society: Ethics and stakeholder management*. Mason: Thomson South-Western.

Carroll, A., Lipartito, K., Post, J., Wherhane, P. & Goodpaster, K. 2012. *Corporate responsibility: The American experience*. Cambridge: Cambridge University Press.

Craig, E. (ed.). 1998. *Routledge encyclopedia of philosophy*. London: Routledge.

Crane, A., Palazzo, G., Spence, L.J. & Matten, D. 2014. Contesting the value of "creating shared value". *California Management Review*, 56(2), 130–153.

Donaldson, T. 1989. *The ethics of international business*. New York: Oxford University Press.

Donaldson, T. 2001. Values in tension: Ethics away from home. In Hoffman, M., Frederick, R. & Schwartz, M. (eds.), *Business ethics: Readings and cases in corporate morality*. Fourth edition. New York: McGraw-Hill, 475–483.

Donaldson, T. 2003. De-compacting the global compact. *Journal of Corporate Citizenship*, 11, 69–72.

Donaldson, T. 2010. *Steps for global transformation: The 2008–2009 economic crisis*. [Online] Available: www.griffith.edu.au/business-commerce/sustainable-enterprise/resources/the-un-global-compact-looking-forward-ten-years-after Accessed: 28 October 2010.

Donaldson, T. 2012. The epistemic fault line in corporate governance. *Academy of Management Review*, 37(2), 256–271.

Donaldson, T. 2021. How values ground value creation: The practical inference framework. *Organization Theory*, 2, 1–27.

Donaldson, T. & Dunfee, T. 1994. Toward a unified conception of business ethics: Integrative social contracts theory. *Academy of Management Review*, 19(2), 252–284.

Donaldson, T. & Dunfee, T. 1999. *Ties that bind: A social contracts approach to business ethics*. Boston: Harvard University Press.

Donaldson, T. & Dunfee, T. 2000a. Précis for: Ties that bind. *Business and Society Review*, 105(4), 436–443.

Donaldson, T. & Dunfee, T. 2000b. Securing the ties that bind: A response to commentators. *Business and Society Review*, 105(4), 480–492.

Donaldson, T. & Walsh, J. 2015. Toward a theory of business. *Research in Organizational Behavior*, 35(181–207). doi:10.1016/j.riob.2015.10.002.

Dunfee, T. 2006. A critical perspective of intregrative social contracts theory: Recurring criticisms and next generation research topics. *Journal of Business Ethics*, 68, 303–328.

Eccles, B., Ioannou, I. & Serafeim, G. 2011. *The impact of a corporate culture of sustainability on corporate behavior and performance*. Working paper no. 12–035. Boston: Harvard Business School.

Eco, U. 1990. *The limits of interpretation*. Bloomington: Indiana University Press.

The Economist. 2005. The good company: A survey of corporate social responsibility, 22 January.

The Economist. 2008. Just good business: A special report on corporate social responsibility, 19 January.

Enderle, G. 1999. *Business ethics in the 21st century walks on two legs*. Amsterdam: Thela Thesis Publishers.

Enderle, G. 2006. Corporate responsibility in the CSR debate. In Wieland, J. (ed.), *Unternehmensethik im Spannungsfeld der Kulturen und Religionen*. Stuttgart: Kohlhammer, 108–124.

Enderle, G. 2007. The ethics of conviction versus the ethics of responsibility: A false antithesis for business ethics. *Journal of Human Values*, 13(2), 83–94.

Enderle, G. 2010. Clarifying the terms of business ethics and CSR. *Business Ethics Quarterly*, 20(4), 730–732.

Enderle, G. 2014. Some ethical explications of the UN framework for business and human rights. In Williams, O.F. (ed.), *Sustainable development*. Notre Dame: University of Notre Dame Press, 163–183.

European Union. 2011. *Green Paper: The EU corporate governance framework*. Brussels. [Online] Available: https://op.europa.eu/en/publication-detail/-/publication/3eed7997-d40b-4984-.

Financial Reporting Council Limited. 2014. *The UK corporate governance code*. [Online] Available: www.frc.org.uk/Our-Work/Publications/Corporate-Governance/UK-Corporate-Governance-Code-2014.pdf Accessed: 14 June 2015.

Freeman, E. 2002. Stakeholder theory of the modern corporation. In Donaldson, T., Cording, M. & Werhane, P. (eds.), *Ethical issues in business: A philosophical approach*. Hoboken, NJ: Prentice Hall, 38–49.

Freeman, E., Harrison, J., Wicks, A., Parmar, B. & De Colle, S. 2010. *Stakeholder theory – The state of the art*. Cambridge: Cambridge University Press.

Freeman, E., Martin, K.E. & Parmar, B.L. 2020. *The power of and: Responsible business without trade-offs*. Columbia University Press.

Friedman, M. 2002. The social responsibility of business is to increase its profits. In Donaldson, T., Cording, M. & Werhane, P. (eds.), *Ethical issues in business: A philosophical approach.* Seventh edition. Hoboken, NJ: Prentice Hall, 33–38.

Garratt, B. 2003. *The fish rots from the Head.* London: Profile Books.

Garratt, B. 2007. Directors and their homework: Developing strategic thought. *International Journal of Business Governance and Ethics*, 3(2), 150–162.

Garratt, B. 2017. *Stop the rot: Reframing governance for directors and politicians.* Abingdon: Routledge.

Garratt, B. 2018. *The four levels of board maturity.* [Online] Available: https://garrattlearningservices.files.wordpress.com/2018/09/four-levels-of-board-maturity-sept-2018.pdf.

Global Reporting Initiative. 2013. *G4 sustainability reporting guidelines.* [Online] Available: www.globalreporting.org/resourcelibrary/GRIG4-Part1-Reporting-Principles-and-Standard-Disclosures.pdf Accessed: 28 November 2014.

Goodpaster, K. & Matthews, J. 1982. Can a corporation have a conscience? *Harvard Business Review*, January/February, 60(1), 132–141.

Grebe, E. & Woermann, M. 2011. *Institutions of integrity and the integrity of institutions: Integrity and ethics in the politics of developmental leadership.* Developmental Leadership Program. [Online] Available: www.dlprog.org/publications/institutions-of-integrity-and-the-integrity-of-institutions-integrity-and-ethics-in-the-politics-of-developmental-leadership.php Accessed: 14 June 2015.

Hall, C. 2007. Are emerging market TNCs sensitive to corporate responsibility issues? *Journal of Corporate Citzenship*, 26, 30–37.

Hilb, M. 2012. *New corporate governance.* Fourth edition. Berlin: Springer.

Hohnen, P. 2010. The United Nations global compact and the global reporting initiative. In Rasche, A. & Kell, G. (eds.), *The United Nations global compact: Achievements, trends and challenges.* New York: Cambridge University Press, 293–313.

Hohnen, P. 2012. *The future of sustainability reporting.* Chatham House. [Online] Available: www.chathamhouse.org/sites/files/chathamhouse/public/Research/Energy,%20Environment%20and%20Development/0112pp_hohnen.pdf Accessed: 14 June 2015.

Hsieh, N.-H. 2004. The obligations of transnational corporations: Rawlsian justice and the duty of assistance. *Business Ethics Quarterly*, 14(4), 643–661.

Hsieh, N.-H. 2006. Voluntary codes of conduct for multinational corporations: Coordinating duties of rescue and justice. *Business Ethics Quarterly*, 16(2), 119–135.

Hsieh, N.-H. 2009a. Corporate social responsibility and the priority of shareholders. *Journal of Business Ethics*, 88, 553–560.

Hsieh, N.-H. 2009b. The normative study of business organizations: A Rawlsian approach. In Smith, J. (ed.), *Normative theory and business ethics.* Lanham: Rowman & Littlefield Publishers Inc., 93–118.

Institute of Directors in Southern Africa. 2016. *The king report on corporate governance in South Africa.* Johannesburg: Institute of Directors in Southern Africa. [Online] Available: www.iodsa.co.za/page/king-iv.

International Corporate Governance Network. 2014. *ICGN global governance principles.* London: International Corporate Governance Network.

Judt, T. 2010. *Ill fares the land.* London: Penguin Books.

Kaptein, M. 2004. Business codes of multinational firms: What do they say? *Journal of Business Ethics*, 50, 13–31.

Kaptein, M. & Wempe, J. 2002. *The balanced company: A theory of corporate integrity.* Oxford: Oxford University Press.

Kell, G. 2012. 12 years later: Reflections on the growth of the UN global compact. *Business & Society*, 52(1), 31–52.

Kell, G. 2013. *Executive director, UN global compact.* New York: Personal interview, 5 August.

Kell, G. & Levin, D. 2003. The global compact network: An historic experiment in learning and action. *Business and Society Review*, 108(2), 151–181.

Kohlberg, L. 1981. *The philosophy of moral development: Moral stages and the idea of justice.* San Francisco: Harper & Row.

KPMG International. 2020. *The time has come. The KPMG survey of sustainability reporting 2020.* [Online] Available: https://assets.kpmg/content/dam/kpmg/xx/pdf/2020/12/the-time-has-come-executive-summary.pdf.

KPMG International. 2022. *KPMG international survey of corporate responsibility reporting 2022.* [Online] Available: https://assets.kpmg/content/dam/kpmg/xx/pdf/2022/10/ssr-small-steps-big-shifts.pdf.

KPMG; UNEP; GRI, Unit for Corporate Governance in Africa. 2010. *Carrots and sticks – Promoting transparency and sustainability: An update on trends in voluntary and mandatory approaches to sustainability reporting.* Amsterdam: Global Reporting Initiative.

Lawton, A. & Páez, I. 2015. Developing a framework for ethical leadership. *Journal of Business Ethics*, 130, 639–649. https://doi.org/10.1007/s10551-014-2244-2.

Leisinger, K. 2007. Capitalism with a human face: The UN global compact. *Journal of Corporate Citizenship*, 28, 1–20.

Malan, D. 2011. Strengthening democracy through governance in Africa – The role of the UN global compact. In Ingley, C. (ed.), *Handbook on emerging issues in corporate governance.* Singapore: World Scientific Publishing Co. Pte Ltd, 217–236.

Malan, D. 2013. The business of business is (responsible) business. In Lawrence, J. & Beamish, P. (eds.), *Globally responsible leadership: Managing according to the UN global compact.* London: Sage Publications Ltd., 21–32.

Malan, D., Taylor, A., Tunkel, A. & Kurtz, B. 2022. *Why business integrity can be a strategic response to ethical challenges.* MIT Sloan Management Review. [Online] Available:https://sloanreview.mit.edu/article/why-business-integrity-can-be-a-strategic-response-to-ethical-challenges/.

McIntosh, M. & Waddock, S. 2010a. Learning from the roundtables on the sustainable enterprise economy: The United Nations Global Compact and the next ten years. In Rasche, A. & Kell, G. (eds.), *The United Nations global compact: Achievements, trends and challenges.* New York: Cambridge University Press, 215–233.

McIntosh, M. & Waddock, S. 2010b. *The UN global compact: Looking forward ten years after.* [Online] Available: www.griffith.edu.au/business-commerce/sustainable-enterprise/resources/the-un-global-compact-looking-forward-ten-years-after Accessed: 28 October 2010.

Newton, L. (ed.). 2004. *Ethics in America: Source reader.* Second edition. Upper Saddle River, NJ (New York, NY): Pearson Education, Inc.

OECD. 2011. *OECD guidelines for multinational enterprises.* [Online] Available: http://mneguidelines.oecd.org/text/ Accessed: 14 June 2015.

Paine, L. 1994. Managing for organizational integrity. *Harvard Business Review*, 72(2), 106–117.

Paine, L., Deshpandé, R., Margolis, D. & Bettcher, K. 2005. Up to code: Does your company's conduct meet world class standards? *Harvard Business Review*, December 2005.

Parfit, D. 2011. *On what matters: Volume 1*. Oxford: Oxford University Press.

Pierce, C. 2010. *Corporate governance in the European union*. Orpington: Global Governance Services Ltd.

Porter, M. & Kramer, M. 2011. Creating shared value. *Harvard Business Review*, Issue HBR Reprint R1101C, 1–17.

Porter, M. & Kramer, M. 2014. A response to Andrew Crane *et al*'s article by Michael E. Porter and Mark R. Kramwer. *California Business Review*, 56(2), 149–151.

Rasche, A. 2010. *The UN global compact – a critique of its critiques*. [Online] Available: www.griffith.edu.au/business-commerce/sustainable-enterprise/resources/the-un-global-compact-looking-forward-ten-years-after Accessed: 28 October 2010.

Rasche, A. & Kell, G. 2010. *The United Nations global compact: Achievements, trends and challenges*. New York: Cambridge University Press.

Rasche, A. & Waddock, S. 2014. Global sustainability governance and the UN Global Compact: A rejoinder to critics. *Journal of Business Ethics*, 122(2), 209–216.

Rawls, J. 1971. *A theory of justice*. Cambridge: Harvard University Press.

Rawls, J. 2001. Justice as fairness. In Hoffman, M., Frederick, R. & Schwartz, M. (eds.), *Business ethics: Readings and cases in corporate morality*. Fourth edition. New York: McGraw-Hill, 53–59.

Rorty, R. 2006. Is philosophy relevant to applied ethics? *Business Ethics Quarterly*, 16(3), 369–380.

Schwab, K. 2008. Global corporate citizenship: Working with governments and civil society. *Foreign Affairs*, January/February, 87(1), 107–118.

Sharbatoghlie, A., Mosleh, M. & Shokatian, T. 2013. Exploring trends in the codes of ethics of the fortune 100 and global 100 corporations. *Journal of Management Development*, 32(7), 675–689.

Smith, J. (ed.). 2009. *Normative theory and business ethics*. Lanham: Rowman & Littlefield.

Smith, K. & Alexander, J. 2013. Which CSR-related headings do fortune 500 companies use on their websites [question mark]. *Business Communication Quarterly*, 76(2), 155–171.

Smurthwaite, M. 2008. The purpose of the corporation. In Williams, O. (ed.), *Peace through commerce: Responsible corporate citizenship and the ideals of the United Nations global compact*. Notre Dame: Notre Dame University Press, 13–55.

Stout, L. 2012. *The shareholder value myth*. Kindle version. Amazon.com Accessed: 15 September 2015.

Taleb, N. 2007. *The Black Swan: The impact of the highly improbable*. London: Penguin Books.

UN Global Compact and Accenture. 2013. *The UN global compact-accenture CEO study on sustainability*. New York: United Nations Global Compact.

UN Global Compact. 2010. *United Nations global compact annual review – anniversary edition*. New York: United Nations Global Compact Office.

UN Principles for Responsible Investment. 2014. *Report on progress 2014*. [Online] Available: http://2xjmlj8428u1a2k5o34l1m71.wpengine.netdna-cdn.com/wp-content/uploads/2014_report_on_progress.pdf Accessed: 14 June 2015.

UNEP, KPMG, GRI & Centre for Corporate Governance in Africa. 2013. *Sustainability reporting policies worldwide – today's best practice, tomorrow's trends*. [Online]

Available: www.governance.usb.ac.za/pdfs/Carrots-and-Sticks.pdf Accessed: 14 June 2015.

UNEP; GRI, University of Stellenbosch Business School. 2020. *Carrots and sticks – sustainability reporting policy: Global trends in disclosure as the ESG agenda goes mainstream*. [Online] Available: www.carrotsandsticks.net.

United Nations. 1987. *Our common future*. [Online] Available: www.un-documents. net/our-common-future.pdf Accessed: 7 December 2014.

United Nations. 1998. *Linking universal values with the global reach of business – strategy note for Davos speech (summary)*. [Online] Available: www.unglobalcompact. org/docs/about_the_gc/GC_Strategy_note_18Dec98.pdf Accessed: 14 December 2014.

United Nations. 2010. *Report of the special representative of the secretary-general on the issue of human rights and corporations and other business enterprises, John Ruggie*. [Online] Available: http://www2.ohchr.org/english/issues/trans_corporations/docs/A-HRC-14-27.pdf Accessed: 2 December 2014.

United Nations. 2011. *Guiding principles on business and human rights*. [Online] Available: www.ohchr.org/Documents/Publications/GuidingPrinciplesBusinessHR_EN.pdf Accessed: 14 June 2015.

United Nations. 2012. *The future we want*. [Online] Available: www.un.org/disabilities/documents/rio20_outcome_document_complete.pdf Accessed: 7 December 2014.

The United Kingdom of Great Britain and Northern Ireland. 2006. Companies act, 2006. [Online]. Available: www.legislation.gov.uk/ukpga/2006/46/pdfs/ukpga_20060046_en.pdf Accessed: 2 October 2019.

U.S. Department of Justice Criminal Division. 2020. *Evaluation of corporate compliance programs*. [Online] Available: www.justice.gov.

Van der Lugt, C. & Malan, D. (eds.). 2012. *Making investment grade: The future of corporate reporting*. Cape Town: United Nations Environment Programme, Deloitte, Centre for Corporate Governance in Africa (University of Stellenbosch Business School).

Visser, W., Matten, D., Pohl, M. & Tolhurst, N. 2007. *The A to Z of corporate social responsibility*. Chichester: John Wiley & Sons Ltd.

Waddock, S. 2013. The future is here for the new CSR: Corporate responsibility and sustainability. In Zollo, M. & Mele, R. (eds.), *The shared value debate: Academic visions on corporate sustainability*. Milan: Egea, 37–46.

Watson, A. 2012. Annual reporting needs to account for more. In Van der Lugt, C. & Malan, D. (eds.), *Making investment grade: The future of corporate reporting*. Cape Town: United Nations Environment Programme, Deloitte, Centre for Corporate Governance in Africa (University of Stellenbosch Business School), 15–18.

Weber, J. & Wasieleski, D. 2013. Corporate ethics and compliance programs: A report, analysis and critique. *Journal of Business Ethics*, 112(2013), 609–626.

Weber, M. 1971 (originally published 1930). *The Protestant ethics and the spirit of capitalism*. Unwin University Book.

Williams, O.F. 2004. The UN global compact: The challenge and the promise. *Business Ethics Quarterly*, 14(4), 755–774.

Williams, O.F. 2008. Responsible corporate citizenship and the ideals of the United Nations global compact. In Williams, O. (ed.), *Peace through commerce: Responsible corporate citizenship and the ideals of the United Nations global compact*. Notre Dame: Notre Dame University Press, 431–552.

Williams, O.F. 2014a. *Corporate social responsibility: The role of business in sustainable development*. New York: Routledge.

Williams, O.F. 2014c. The United Nations global compact: What did it promise? *Journal of Business Ethics*, 122(2), 241–251.

Willliams, O.F. 2014b. *Sustainable development: The UN millennium development goals, the UN global compact and the common good*. Notre Dame: University of Notre Dame Press.

World Economic Forum. 2013. *A new social covenant*. [Online] Available: http://www3.weforum.org/docs/WEF_GAC_NewSocialCovenant_Report_2014.pdf Accessed: 14 June 2015.

World Economic Forum. 2021. *The rise and role of the chief integrity officer*. [Online] Available: https://www3.weforum.org/docs/WEF_The_Rise_and_Role_of_the_Chief_Integrity_Officer_2021.pdf.

Zollo, M. & Mele, R. (eds.). 2013. *The shared value debate: Academic visions on corporate sustainability*. Milan: Egea.

Index

responsibility: amoral model 26;
autonomy model 26–27;
commitment to taking
52–53, *53*, 54–57; concept
of 25–26; ethical leadership
and 52–55, 56–57; ethics of
54–55; functional model 26;
governance and 58, *59*, *60*;
hypernorms and 122;
managing 58, *59*, 74, *74*, 75;
moral 25; power and 15, 25;
purpose and 5; reporting and
93–94, *94*, 98; understanding
14; value and 5; *see also* moral
responsibility
right of voice 41, 41n15
Rijksmuseum 1, 3
Rio+20 Earth Summit 96, 114
Rorty, R. 46
Rousseau, J.-J. 31–32
Ruggie, J. 21, **21**

Scanlon, T. 28
Schapiro, M. 99
Schwab, K. 16–17
secondary moral actor theory 26
Secret and Swift Messenger, The
(Wilkins) 3
Serafeim, G. 98
social audits 93
social contract theory: changes in values
45–47; citizen-government
contracts and 38; concept of
30–32; inequality and 33;
normative theory and 29, 36;
see also Integrative Social
Contracts Theory (ISCT);
stakeholder theory
society: burdened 27; business
relationship with 15–17;
human beings and 7; impact
of corporations on 25–26, 36,
101; organisations and 7; social
responsibility and 18; well-
ordered 27
spiritual leadership 56
stakeholder capitalism 68
Stakeholder Capitalism Metrics 104
stakeholders: compliance and 12, 76;
corporate behaviour and 12;
corporate governance and 61;
corporate responsibility and 21,
24, 75; corporations as 16–17;

definition of 34; social contracts
and 35, 40; sustainability
reporting and 98–99
stakeholder statutes 87
stakeholder theory: CSR/CR and 15;
deontology and 30; Doctrine of
Fair Contracts and 35–36; ISCT
and 40, 42–43; as pragmatic
approach 73; primary/secondary
stakeholders in 34, *35*; rules of
the game and 36; shareholder
interests and 29, 33–34;
stakeholder groups in 34, *35*;
tenets of 34–35
standards: compliance and 12; corporate
governance and 60, 64–66;
ethical 55–56; ethics codes and
87; European 67–68; global
organisations and 68–71, 95,
97–98, 100–104, 109, **111**,
112–116, 118–120; mandatory
vs. voluntary 11, 106–110,
112, 119; reporting and 97–98,
100–105; sanctions and 110,
110n3, 112; sustainability
reporting and 94–95, 97–100;
voluntary initiatives and
52–53, 100, 106–109, 116,
118–120
Stanford Research Institute 34
strategic thinking 61–62
structural hypernorms 41
substantive hypernorms 41
sustainability: advancement of 107–108;
business performance and 67,
71, 94–95; concept of 71,
72; corporate responsibility
(CR) and 8; ESG and 71, 73;
reporting and 93–99, 101, 105;
triple bottom line approach
(TBL/3BL) *72*, 73, 95
SustainAbility (think tank) 94–95
Sustainability Accounting Standards
Board (SASB) 95, 100
sustainable development 8, 71, 73
Sustainable Development Goals (SDGs):
compared to MDGs **112–113**,
115, **120**; duty of assistance
and 27; infographic for *115*;
proposed goals 114–115;
UN approval of 115; UN
development of 114; voluntary
standards and 109, **111**, 112

Printed in the United States
by Baker & Taylor Publisher Services